John Leonard Wilson
Confessor for the Faith

Conducted wedding of
WS Ainslie and J M Carr
organist at Eighton Banks.

John Leonard Wilson
Confessor for the Faith

by
ROY McKAY

HODDER AND STOUGHTON
LONDON · SYDNEY · AUCKLAND · TORONTO

Preface

I wish to acknowledge my debt to all those who have helped me with their personal recollections whose names are mentioned in the text.

I am grateful to Mrs. Wilson, at whose request I undertook the writing of the book. She has given me valuable information on many of the events recorded, and made available to me a large number of documents. Among these were Press cuttings from which I have quoted a few extracts. These are named in the text as having appeared in *The Birmingham Post*, *The Birmingham Teachers' Journal*, *The Sunday Times Magazine*, and *John Bull*.

I have to thank the Reverend John Hayter for putting at my disposal his diaries kept during the years he was with Leonard Wilson in Singapore, and for much other help over this period. Canon Leslie Wilson kindly allowed me to draw on his records of the Wilson family, which made possible the account given of Leonard's parents and grandparents. Miss Brenda Holloway provided me with a diary of events for the Birmingham years and other important background information for this period. Mr. James Wilson has been most generous of his time and thought in reading and sorting a large number of the documents. I am grateful to Canon David Edwards for his wise counsel; and to Miss Joan Bowman for her patience and accuracy in preparing a fair copy of the text.

Finally I wish to thank my wife, who helped me to gather the material for the book. Her interest, critical judgment and encouragement have been a continuing strength and support during the writing of it.

May 1972   ROY MCKAY

Contents

John Leonard Wilson
Confessor for the Faith

CHAPTER 1

Singapore:
Before Internment

ON OCTOBER 10th, 1943, soon after dawn, the civilians who were interned in Changi Prison, Singapore, were called out to parade in the main yard. They had no reason to suppose that this was more than one of the routine roll-calls. However, it soon became obvious that something very different was afoot. The Japanese military police, the notorious Kampetai, had arrived in force and were taking over the camp. A number of the internees were called out by name, labelled and segregated from the main body, and taken away by the police to their headquarters in Singapore, which had been set up in a building which had formerly been the Y.M.C.A. centre. Here they were confined in appalling cell conditions, and the military police began their interrogations under torture. These interrogations went on for many months.

Leonard Wilson, then Bishop of Singapore, was taken by the police on October 17th, the day before he was to have held a Confirmation service in the camp. He was questioned under torture on that evening and during most of the day on October 18th and 19th. When he was returned to his cell on the third evening, he was in a semi-conscious state, in which he remained for three weeks.

This experience was in many ways central to Leonard Wilson's life. Not only did the story become one of the

Christian epics of the century, but, more importantly, he himself regarded these events as among the most significant moments of his own Christian experience, and a lasting proof of the reality of the Christian faith. That is the reason why this narrative begins with the account of his time in Singapore, before and during internment.

In January 1941, Cosmo Lang, Archbishop of Canterbury, wrote to Leonard Wilson, then Dean of Hong Kong, offering him the Bishopric of Singapore. Bishop Roberts had resigned, and been appointed Warden of St. Augustine's College, Canterbury. The archbishop said that, in the event of Leonard's acceptance, he would have to consider the difficult question of the place of his consecration. There were legal difficulties about authorising a consecration outside England, but if wartime conditions made it impossible for Leonard to make the journey home, he would have to take the risk of authorising a consecration either at Hong Kong or at Singapore.

The archbishop was anxious to avoid delay and asked Leonard to cable his answer. As the archbishop's letter had been posted in Canterbury with a twopenny stamp, it is not surprising that there was some delay in his receiving a reply, and Leonard must have been somewhat mystified on receiving a cable from the archbishop saying, 'Why haven't you answered my letter?' when, in fact, no letter had arrived. By March 17th Leonard had made up his mind to accept, and he wrote to the Council of the Cathedral at Hong Kong, so that they would be the first to hear of his decision. At the time he noted down his own feelings for and against acceptance. The reasons for going were: the archbishop, Bishop Hall, and his friends all thought he ought to; it was 'No good praying for a spirit of adventure and hardship and sacrifice, if not prepared to make any effort'. He listed his qualifications as: 'Administration. Pastor Pastorum. Government or political interest. This last important for the future.' He noted the following reasons against going: 'Climate. Education of children. Churchmanship. Contract in

Hong Kong. Lack of friends. Lack of spiritual discipline. Infirmity of temper and passion. Responsibility and loneliness.' As a footnote he added, 'Unworthy thoughts!' He also added, 'Would like the significance of being a bishop. It would give my father no end of a kick. Might even later be offered something more congenial.'

After his appointment, but before his consecration, Leonard made a brief visit to Singapore. He attended morning service in the cathedral, wearing a collar and tie. The Reverend John Hayter, who was taking the service, was not sure how a bishop-elect, thus attired, ought to be treated, and decided against including a prayer for him. This omission did not go unremarked by Leonard. It was a small matter, but it illustrated an action and reaction which was typical. Leonard knew that he was coming to a diocese with a High Church tradition, where conformity in clerical dress would be taken for granted, but he had a strong compulsion in such situations to stick his neck out: hence the collar and tie. However, that did not mean that he was not to be recognised as the bishop-elect.

Shortly afterwards he wrote to an old friend, Canon Jack Bennitt:

I did most sincerely hope that the job would not be offered to me, but having been offered by the Archbishop and having received unanimous advice from those whose counsels I sought, I felt it was my duty to accept. I hope it is not too severe a blow to the clergy of the diocese. I am grateful to you for all your help, and it is good to know that I have at least one friend amongst the clergy there.

In a letter to another old friend, the Reverend Jock Malcolm, he wrote:

It seems to be rather a spiky diocese, and already there seem to be resignations because of my modernism. I think three or four of the clergy will stay to fulfil their contracts if nothing else, and it may not be so bad as one or two reports make out.

Whatever misgivings Leonard may have had, his heart must have been greatly warmed by the cable he received from his father, 'You are well qualified. Accept. Loving wishes. Dad Wilson.'

On July 22nd, the anniversary of his wedding, Leonard was consecrated in St. John's Cathedral, Hong Kong. The presiding bishop was the American Bishop of Manilla, Norman Binstead, and he was assisted by R. O. Hall, Bishop of Hong Kong, and a Chinese bishop, C. T. Sung. A few days later Leonard and his wife left for Singapore.

Bishop Hall had been booked some months earlier for a lecture tour in America. When the archbishop's cable had arrived, Leonard had said to Bishop Hall, 'I will only accept so long as you don't, as a result, cancel your lecture tour in America.' Bishop Hall went, and the bombing of Pearl Harbor took place before the tour was ended. It was four years before he heard any news of Leonard. He was on the platform of Redhill station, and read a newspaper headline over the shoulder of a commuter which said, 'Tortured bishop prays for his enemies.' It was the first news out of a liberated Singapore.

Leonard and his family were settled in Bishopsbourne by the beginning of August. It was only four months to the Japanese invasion. The first two months he spent in Singapore, and the last two touring the diocese. He got back to Singapore on December 9th, the day after the Japanese had begun landing operations at Kota Bahru, a town on the east coast near the Siamese border, and Pearl Harbor had been bombed. The story of the rapid march of disastrous events which followed in horrifying succession, until the surrender of Singapore on February 15th, 1942, is here only our concern in so far as they affected Leonard and his work.

Mary Wilson, and their three children, Susan, Timothy and Martin, were with Leonard at Bishopsbourne until January 16th, when they left for Australia. Their house had become a temporary home for women and children who had come down

16

from farther north as the Japanese advanced. Then, as always, Leonard and Mary had a great gift for hospitality. In spite of the growing threat of the advance they remained cheerful and serene, and made a very happy Christmas for their full house of refugee guests.

The day after his family left, Leonard was sitting at his desk, in an office in the suburbs of Singapore, dipping into *The Oxford Book of English Verse*, when a young captain announced himself, and, in somewhat angry tones, asked him what he was doing for the war effort. Leonard had spent the morning helping in the evacuation of women and children who were leaving for Australia and South Africa. He had witnessed much sorrow and a great deal of courage, and he was alone, without his family, in a place he had only lived in for a few weeks.

This was the sort of situation which called out Leonard's fighting instinct, and he answered the slightly insulting question by saying he represented the civilisation for which the captain was fighting. However, the captain's question made him wonder where, in fact, he could be most useful in the coming days. He had lost seven-eighths of his diocese, and the future was completely uncertain. He decided to apply for a chaplaincy, and the same afternoon went to see the Assistant Chaplain-General, who referred it to the General in command. The latter felt it might be awkward having a diocesan bishop as a chaplain, and suggested that Leonard should be gazetted as a volunteer, which would limit his service to Malaya. He was duly appointed Chaplain Second Class, and for a short time this was a useful arrangement, which gave him official access to several military hospitals. However, a few weeks later, two or three days before the surrender of Singapore, the chaplain advised Leonard to take off his army chaplain's badge and revert to being a civilian.

Mary Wilson made her way with the children to Bowral, in New South Wales, where there were a number of families who had been evacuated from Hong Kong or Singapore. Here their

17

youngest son, James, was born in September. It was eighteen months before Mary had any news of Leonard. Then a postcard arrived, sent from Changi. This contained just ordinary remarks, saying he was well, and hoping that she was, and asking after the children, and then ended with the words, 'Interesting news at the end of a letter from Col. Paul Moffatt.' Years later he told her that he knew she had a crossword-puzzle mind, and would work it out. She found her way to the final verses of the Epistle to the Colossians in Moffatt's translation, and read, 'This salutation is in my own hand. Remember I am in prison. Grace be with you.'

In the last few days before the surrender, Singapore Cathedral was turned into a hospital for Australian soldiers. Leonard had offered it to the R.A.M.C. Some of the wounded died there, and were buried in the cathedral grounds. The city was in the utmost state of confusion, and bombing and shelling were more or less continuous. Leonard and John Hayter, who had joined him at Bishopsbourne a week before the surrender, and was to be with him for the next twenty months, moved first to St. Andrew's Hospital, and then to the general hospital on the night of the surrender. Three days later this had to be evacuated, and they moved to a part of the mental hospital some way out of the town.

Two events of these terrible days show something of Leonard's attitude and spirit. Among those living at Bishopsbourne at Christmas time were Canon and Mrs. Bennitt. Bennitt was Chinese Missioner for the Society for the Propagation of the Gospel. After the Japanese had crossed on to the mainland, Leonard found that two tyres of his car were punctured, and there was no one to mend them. Bennitt told Leonard that he had seen a wrecked car of the same make near the airport, and its wheels might do. They waited until the bombardment let up a bit, and then went in Bennitt's car and collected two wheels off the wrecked car, and fitted them on. As things seemed quiet, they decided to drive on to the village of Siglap, a few miles farther east, where they knew of a bakery. They collected a large quantity of bread and returned to the hospital. The people at the hospital said they could not have been to Siglap as this was outside the perimeter, and they would have had to cross the Japanese lines twice. They said they had certainly been there, and the Japanese were evidently not where the authorities thought they were.

During the three days Leonard was at the mental hospital, he disappeared for a large part of two of them with a driver and an ambulance, and came back in the evening to the hospital with the ambulance full of medical supplies and food which he had purloined from a variety of places. But the time for such exploits was short, and before the week was out the Japanese had issued the order by which all civilians not employed in essential services were to be interned. After long arguments the authorities agreed that Leonard and two of his clergy, John Hayter and the Reverend Sorby Adams, should not be interned, and all three returned to Bishopsbourne. They remained free for the next thirteen months. All the other European clergy and diocesan workers were interned.

For the period during which they were at liberty, very little restriction was placed on the movements of Leonard, Hayter and Adams. At the beginning of December, Hayter and Adams signed a form of parole which bound them to be indoors by 8.30 p.m., but Leonard was not required to do this. Their return to Bishopsbourne and freedom of activity were largely due to the good offices of a Japanese officer, Lieutenant Ogawa. Ogawa was an Anglican who attended the cathedral regularly. He arrived in Singapore soon after the occupation, where he held the position of Director of Religion and Education. It was Ogawa who obtained permission from the authorities for Leonard to visit prisoner-of-war camps without an escort for the purpose of taking confirmation services. He gave Leonard a letter in Japanese which explained who the bishop was, the nature of confirmation, and requested opportunities for

Leonard to visit the camps, 'to cheer the spirits of the prisoners'. In the early days of this time at Bishopsbourne, Leonard and Ogawa had a number of private meetings, but these were abandoned when they both felt that they were arousing the suspicion of the Japanese military police.

Adams recalls how Ogawa secured his freedom when he had been arrested by the Japanese. Passing along the Kim Seng Road, Adams heard the voice of a fellow-Australian, a prisoner-of-war, from the other side of a fence, 'Got a cigarette, mate?' Having a tin of fifty, given to him half an hour previously, he threw it over the fence. This action was seen by a guard, and Adams was arrested and taken off to prison. On his way there he was seen by some friends, who reported to Leonard. Leonard started at once to make inquiries, but without success. He then went to Ogawa, who intervened on Adams's behalf, secured his release, and gave his personal guarantee to the military police for Adams's future good conduct. Adams writes, 'Whatever else I remember of Leonard, the most vivid recollection is the sight of his welcoming open arms on my return that day from the military police.'

The fact that Leonard stayed out of internment so long was largely due to the good offices of Ogawa, who held his post until September, when he was transferred to Sumatra. Leonard himself wrote at a later date:

Ogawa was extremely useful in seeing that there was religious liberty. He was also useful in seeing that religious buildings were respected. His task was not always easy, because the military police were suspicious of his Christian interests, and he took a courageous stand on this point. On May 24th, which was Whitsunday, permission was given for a sermon which I preached, and Ogawa read the lessons in English. (There was no ban on church services, but sermons were prohibited.) After he went to Sumatra, life became a little more difficult, and the Japanese authorities were suspicious of our contacts with the Asiatic population, and began to warn neutrals and others to have nothing to do with the bishop and his European clergy.

Within a few weeks of their return to Bishopsbourne, Leonard, Adams and Hayter had settled down to something of a regular life. All payments of salary had ceased with the fall of Singapore, but throughout their thirteen months before internment they were supported entirely with gifts of food, money and clothing, from their fellow Christians and from Jews. They received nothing in pay or rations from the Japanese authorities. Leonard's Chinese houseboy, Ah Sing, returned, and stayed with them until they were taken to Changi. In the evenings they often played three-handed bridge, the bidder to take the dummy hand, which remained hidden. Leonard was in the top class as a bridge-player, and he could not suffer kindly those who were less skilful at the game. Those who were competent enjoyed playing with him; those who were not suffered the usual agonies. Mr. Geoffrey Folliott writes:

I have very vivid memories of many very happy games I played when we were interned in Changi prison. The usual four were Leonard, John Hayter, Sorby Adams and myself. I always tell my bridge-playing friends (and I still play a lot of bridge), that Leonard was the finest player I have ever played with. He was a fantastic psychologist and seemed to know, especially when he was holding poor cards, exactly how far he could push his opponents to overcall. He almost seemed to be able to see through one's cards.

Adams writes:

I remember that Leonard always preserved the same interval, of about two seconds, before playing any card, whether that card had any significance or not. No opponent could then learn, from either speed or hesitation in play, any extra matter about his hand.

Bridge, a joint reading of *Cold Comfort Farm*, and a pitch and putt course in the garden, inspired by a friend of Adams's, a soft drinks manufacturer, who visited them once a week, these were their lighter moments in a life which was always uncertain. For most of the day they were busy in looking after the needs of their Christian congregations in Singapore, maintaining regular services of worship, and doing all they could to strengthen morale. From the first Leonard realised that his own days of freedom might be limited, and he was determined to do all he could in the time left to him to build up the life of the Church in Singapore, so that it could continue its work on its own resources through the difficult days ahead. There is no doubt that the personal friendships he made during this time, with those connected with the different Christian communities in Singapore, played a large part in stabilising the situation, and in laying the foundations for the time when the war was over.

As always, adversity had brought the different Christian Churches closer together, and Leonard, who all his life was devoted to the cause of Christian unity, made the fullest use of the opportunities the wartime situation had created. In June a Federation of Christian Churches was formed, and Leonard sent out a circular letter to all with whom he could get in touch. Members of the Council represented the following Christian bodies: Anglicans, Methodists, Presbyterians, Adventists, Brethren, Salvation Army, Pentecostal, Syrian, Far Eastern Missionary, and Overseas Baptists. The President was the Reverend D. D. Chelliah, an Indian who had been Adams's chief assistant at St. Andrew's Boys' School, of which Adams had been the Principal. At the time of the surrender Leonard had appointed Chelliah to be in charge of the diocese in the event of his being interned. After the fall of Singapore, the Japanese appointed Chelliah to be senior assistant to the Director of Religion and Education, Ogawa. This was a difficult position which Chelliah filled with great tact, and he was able to do much in calling the attention of the Japanese authorities to the needs of the Churches. From the time that Leonard was interned, Chelliah carried the responsibility for the work at the cathedral and for the rest of the diocese.

In his circular letter about the Federation of Christian Churches, Leonard drew attention to the importance of the two main committees; one for social service, the other for union. He wrote:

Their work is urgent and, in the case of social service, immediate. But relief work must of necessity be local, and organised to meet needs as they arise. I want therefore in this letter, to emphasise the work of the second committee, of which I have been invited to be chairman. There are few subjects which have taken up so much of my thoughts and prayers in the last ten years as the subject of union: so I welcome every opportunity and occasion to bring it to the thoughtful notice of Christians. The atheism, secularism and anti-Christian faiths of the western world are the greatest menace. I am amazed at the indifference of so many Christians to the purpose of their religion. We are supposed to be the light of the world and the salt of the earth. May God forgive our dimness and insipidity! Our first task is to arouse interest in union, and to set up machinery whereby the whole question may be studied.

There is no doubt there will be much heart searching and perhaps painful agitation. Our complacency will be disturbed and the foundation of our faith may have to be re-examined. It may be that some of our cherished convictions are seen to be prejudices, and most of us will be asked to sacrifice customs which are greatly loved, for the sake of a united witness to our faith. Our aim is a Universal Church in Malaya, not uniformity of worship but a united faith, and an agreed order of ministry. One of the steps to such a goal is a Federation of Christian Churches.

The Federation held monthly united services. There were

meetings for discussion and the exchange of ideas, and much was done through the Federation's committee to help meet the needs of the destitute of whatever race or creed. This latter work had the support of the Japanese authorities, and the Federation, together with other voluntary bodies, received some financial help from the Japanese Government.

As has already been mentioned, Leonard was able, through the good offices of Ogawa, to visit most of the prisoner-of-war camps, and he held confirmations in a number of them. One of these camps, a smaller one, was not included in the list to which Leonard had access; but, as this particular camp had no resident chaplain, it was important that it should be visited. As soon as Leonard heard about it, he drove out there and was allowed to enter without demur by the Japanese guards. This was the first of many regular weekly visits for a communion service.

It was through his contact with this camp that Leonard was able to establish a system of messages between those in prisoner-of-war camps and their relatives or friends in the civilian intern-ment camp at Changi. It was Japanese policy throughout the whole period of the occupation to allow no communication between the civilians and the prisoners-of-war. From the start of internment certain classes of civilian patients were allowed by the Japanese to be taken to the Japanese-named Miyako Hos-pital, formerly the General Hospital, which was centred in the buildings which had been used as the mental hospital. Here these civilian patients from Changi were put in special wards set aside for them. From the beginning, Leonard, Hayter and Adams had been allowed to visit this hospital. Once Leonard had established his right to enter the small prisoner-of-war camp, it became possible to arrange an exchange of letters through the internee wards in Miyako Hospital and this camp. These letters could be passed on by this camp to other prisoner-of-war camps with which it was in constant contact. It was due to Leonard's initiative that a great many prisoners and internees thus heard news of relatives and friends, which they would not

24

otherwise have received. Undoubtedly he and the others took serious personal risks in arranging these exchanges, but the Japanese never discovered what was going on, and Leonard was not questioned about it, when he was later under interrogation by the military police.

It was through this exchange of messages that Leonard learnt that the internees in Changi were in need of funds. Many of them had taken large sums of money with them into internment. This money was not taken from them by the Japanese. A camp committee, elected by the men themselves, set up a common fund and invited loans to it, which would be repaid after the war. The money was used for the purchase of food and medical supplies in the town, and this was done through the Japanese. However, the original fund, and additions to it by those who came into internment later, were insufficient to meet the camp's needs. The diet provided by the Japanese was very defective, and additions to it were specially necessary for the sick, children, and the older internees.

A message was got to Leonard through the hospital and he set about collecting funds. He was able to borrow money in the name of the Anglican Church. Much of it came from the Chinese who believed in the final success of the British, and were ready to lend money in return for I.O.U.s. The money had to be smuggled into the camp without arousing suspicion, and a number of different methods were employed to do this. While Leonard was still at liberty it was comparatively easy to find ways of getting the money in, but when Leonard, Hayter and Adams were interned at the end of March 1943, it became much more difficult.

When Leonard knew his internment was imminent, he arranged with his Indian secretary, K. T. Alexander, that, on receiving a message from him, he was to go to a prearranged rendezvous, borrow the money, and hand it over to a young Chinese couple, Choy Koon Heng and his wife Elizabeth Choy. This plan worked, and money came into the camp up to the time that the military police took control on October 10th. There were people who came out of Changi under guard for various reasons. Lorries, driven by internees, came into the town to buy goods and equipment for the camp. Some of these were supplied by a shop in Albert Street, near which a Chinese called Ah Tek had his own shop. The Choys passed money over to Ah Tek, and the lorry drivers, who had been instructed in the plan, made an opportunity to pick it up from him while the lorries were being loaded.

Norman Coulson, an engineer, who was not interned until the middle of 1943, took enormous risks to help both the civilians in Changi, and the prisoners-of-war. He had remained free as one engaged in essential services, and he made many visits as part of his engineering duties. He used these to bring in stores and extra equipment for the internees, and he also arranged to collect B.B.C. news items and get them into the camp. On one occasion he concealed a large sum of the borrowed money in a piece of piping which he was taking to the camp. Another way used to smuggle in the money was found by Leonard and other clergy who were on funeral duty. Money was put in the all-purpose coffin when it was returned empty from the cemetery. Sometimes money was put in Leonard's robe case, while he was taking a funeral.

Many of those engaged in these smuggling operations suffered for their humanity and courage. Norman Coulson, whose story is one of the epics of the period, was among those taken to the military police headquarters. He died as a result of the treatment he received. The Choys, Ah Tek, and Alexander were all arrested, and Ah Tek died from the same cause. Leonard's share in the business was one of the grounds for his own torture by the military police.

When Ogawa left for Sumatra in September 1942, things became increasingly difficult for Leonard and the others. In the middle of that month they had to leave Bishopsbourne, and found refuge in a friend's house in Dyson Road. The circum-

26

stances of their being moved were curious. In the garden of Bishopsbourne there was a Flame of the Forest tree. Leonard thought this had become unsafe, and, if it fell, it might damage the house. He therefore took steps to have the tree cut down. The Japanese authorities got to hear of this, and a great row followed. At the time Leonard could not understand what the row was about, and he took as strong a line as he could to preserve his rights. However, it was made clear to Leonard and the others that they had got to get out, and there were long arguments about what they could take with them. Hayter recalled in his diary:

> Eventually the bishop bade the invaders farewell and left them in possession, but not before the interpreter, who had been to see us several times, patted him on the shoulder and said, 'I am very sorry this had to happen to you, very sorry.' This was a striking example of the contrast between the official and the individual, since it was he who had previously been shouting the odds.

It was not until some time later that they discovered the reason for their being turned out. The Japanese general was an Animist, and his faith would not allow him to see execution done on the Flame of the Forest tree.

When Christmas came, the churches kept the festival and were attended by large congregations. There was a Boxing Night party at St. Hilda's Mission Church at Katong, of which Hayter was in charge, when Leonard gave a magnificent rendering of 'I Was a Pale Young Curate Then'. On the Sunday after Christmas there was a united service of nine lessons and carols in the cathedral, when the congregation numbered over a thousand.

But the days of freedom were numbered, and on March 27th, 1943, Leonard and his two companions were given forty-eight hours' notice that they were to go to Changi. Leonard took what final steps he could to insure the continuance of church life.

One of these was to ordain as deacon and priest, at twenty-four hours' notice, John Handy, who had helped Hayter at St. Hilda's as a licensed lay-reader. Leonard put him in charge of St. Hilda's, while he continued in his secular work at the Chinese Bank.

After the Sunday evening services and farewells on March 28th, Leonard and his companions spent the rest of the time packing stores they intended to take in with them, and checking large sums of cash which they had collected. Sorby Adams recalls, 'The Japanese did not seem to take any notice of what we took in, and the two lorries were piled high, and our pockets were full of cash. On the top of one load sat Leonard with a top hat on his head, as we went through the gates of the prison in triumph.' The internees who witnessed this scene were not amused by the top hat. It was an example of the way in which Leonard sometimes failed to sense a situation, or perhaps he did sense it, and refused then, as in earlier days, to subscribe to the idea that new boys should not make themselves conspicuous.

CHAPTER 2

Singapore: Internment

THERE WERE AT THIS time about three thousand people interned in Changi. The conditions were squalid and the diet inadequate, but on the whole life was not unbearable. Sir Norman Alexander, who had been Professor of Physics at Raffles University, and went into Changi with the first group of internees, recalls that many of these were highly educated and senior people in their professions, or they would not have been on the reserved list. About one hundred and twenty different subjects were taught in the camp in small groups, and there was a library of three thousand books. They had quiz sessions, when questions were sent in beforehand on any subject and answered by experts in the camp. Leonard took his turn with these in dealing with questions of religion. There were lectures, plays, games, concerts and gramophone recitals.

It was due to this self-discipline and effort on the part of those interned that morale in the camp remained so high. However, nothing could alter the fact that they were living in appallingly confined conditions, with insufficient rations, and cut off from family and friends, for news of whom many waited months and years. The situation was a cruel and hard test of courage and endurance.

Church services were held regularly. When Leonard and his companions arrived, the routine was well established. Archdeacon Graham White, who had been in Singapore for many years and latterly had been in charge of the cathedral, had five other clergy with him: G. B. Thompson, Colin King, Jack Bennitt, Bernard Eales and Eric Scott. Many people had tried to persuade the archdeacon and Mrs. Graham White to leave before the surrender, but they were adamant in their refusal. Both died in internment early in 1945. It was the archdeacon and his fellow clergy who had made the arrangements for religious services in the camp, and there was a large measure of co-operation between them and other Christian denominations. When Leonard and the others came in, they took their share in the existing arrangements.

Everything changed on October 10th, 1943, when the military police descended on Changi and took over control. The question naturally arises as to the grounds upon which Leonard was among those taken to their headquarters for questioning. The commission which was appointed immediately after liberation in the autumn of 1945, of which Sir Norman Alexander was a member, took statements from thirty-six survivors of those arrested by the military police. Their report, published on September 3rd of that year, stated:

> The course of the interrogation showed that the Japanese were trying to establish that there was a spy organisation in Changi prison which received and transmitted by radio telephone; which had established contacts in the town for the purpose of sabotage and stirring up anti-Japanese feeling; and which collected money from outside for this purpose. In fact, there was no spy organisation, no radio transmission and no attempt to promote anti-Japanese activities outside the camp. There were, however, radio-receiving sets in the camp which were used solely for the reception of news, and money was collected from outside the camp for the sole purpose of supplementing the totally inadequate rations supplied by the Japanese.

It seems certain that the military police had got to know that money was being brought into the camp, and that Leonard was implicated in this. Leonard himself thought their suspicions were increased by the discovery among his papers of some lectures he had given on T. E. Lawrence. He referred to this in his broadcast in October 1946, when he said, 'Many of you will remember that part of Lawrence's work, a very small part, was the using of money to influence the Arab leaders to revolt against the Turks. They seemed to imagine that I was carrying out the same policy, and trying to stir up the local population to revolt against the conquering Japanese.'

John Hayter recorded the following account of Leonard's torture. It was based on what Leonard told him after his return to the camp hospital.

In the evening of his arrival Leonard was questioned, the interrogation being punctuated with beatings, for between three and four hours. On the following morning he was again taken to the torture room, where he was made to kneel down. A three angled bar was placed behind his knees. He was then made to kneel on his haunches. His hands were tied behind his back and pulled up to a position between his shoulder blades. His head was forced down and he remained in this position for seven and a half hours. Any attempt to ease the strain from the cramp in his thighs was frustrated by the guards, who brought the flat of their hobnailed boots down hard on to his thighs. At intervals the bar between his knees would be twisted, or the guards would jump on to one or both projecting ends. Beatings and kicks were frequent. Throughout the whole of this time he was being questioned and told that he was a spy. This was one of the times when he lost his nerve and pleaded for death.

Again, the next morning, he was brought up from the cells, and this time tied face upwards to a table with his head hanging over the end of it. For several hours he remained in that position while relays of soldiers beat him systematically from the ankles to the thighs with three-fold knotted ropes. He fainted, was revived with warm milk, and then the beating was continued. He estimated that he must have received over three hundred lashes. The beating, he said, was far easier to bear than the excruciating pain of the previous day. It was not long before he lost all sense of feeling. The blows had lost their power to hurt, so dead were the nerves of his body. Finally he was taken down to the cells and thrown on the floor. There was no skin left on the front of his legs from his thighs downwards. He had no medical attention while he was in that state, and he said that if it had not been for the help of Stephenson, a fellow internee in his cell, who subsequently died from the treatment he himself received, he would not have survived.

Leonard never dwelt on the physical horror of the torture he suffered. When he referred to this time, it was to make clear that this experience had established for him once and for all the truth of the Christian faith he confessed. As the story of his earlier years unfolds, it will be seen that he did not always possess that quiet assurance of those who can say, 'I am not ashamed: for I know Him whom I have believed.' After the experience of those days of horror, pain and darkness, he knew that he had been upheld by God's love beyond the point of no return, and whatever doubts and difficulties, failures and disappointments, later came his way, his spirit was never defeated, for now he too could say with quiet confidence, 'I know Him whom I have believed.'

It was on October 13th, 1946, three years after these events, that Leonard preached in the Sunday service of the B.B.C., and first gave to the world some account of what the experiences of those days had come to mean to him. He said:

I remember Archbishop William Temple in one of his books writing that if you pray for any particular virtue, whether it be patience or courage or love, one of the answers God gives to you is an opportunity for exercising that virtue.

After my first beating I was almost afraid to pray for courage lest I should have another opportunity for exercising it, but my unspoken prayer was there, and without God's help I doubt whether I could have come through. Long hours of ignoble pain were a severe test. In the middle of that torture they asked me if I still believed in God. When, by God's help, I said, 'I do,' they asked me why God did not save me, and by the help of his Holy Spirit, I said, 'God does save me. He does not save me by freeing me from pain or punishment, but he saves me by giving me the spirit to bear it.' And when they asked me why I did not curse them, I told them that it was because I was a follower of Jesus Christ, who taught us that we were all brethren. I did not like to use the words, 'Father, forgive them.' It seemed too blasphemous to use our Lord's words, but I felt them, and I said, 'Father, I know these men are doing their duty. Help them to see that I am innocent.' And when I muttered, 'Forgive them,' I wondered how far I was being dramatic and if I really meant it, because I looked at their faces as they stood around and took it in turn to flog, and their faces were hard and cruel and some of them were evidently enjoying their cruelty. But by the grace of God I saw those men not as they were, but as they had been. Once they were little children playing with their brothers and sisters and happy in their parents' love, in those far-off days before they had been conditioned by their false nationalist ideals, and it is hard to hate little children; but even that was not enough. There came into my mind, as I lay on the table, the words of that communion hymn:

> Look, Father, look on His anointed face,
> And only look on us as found in Him;
> Look not on our misusings of Thy grace,
> Our prayer so languid, and our faith so dim;
> For lo! between our sins and their reward
> We set the Passion of Thy Son our Lord.

And so I saw them, not as they were, not as they had been, but as they were capable of becoming, redeemed by the power of Christ, and I knew it was only common sense to say, 'Forgive.'

While Leonard did not suffer further physical torture, except for one brief period, the interrogation went on for months. Two other stories serve to show something of the strangeness of the Japanese attitude of mind. At one period of the interrogation, Leonard was asked each day how old he was. He said he was forty-five. Then one day when he was asked the same question, he answered, 'I am forty-six.' The guards immediately broke out in chorus, 'You are lying; you are lying. You told us you were forty-five.' Leonard said, 'I am not lying, because today is my birthday.' The atmosphere changed at once. The guards made him comfortable, gave him food and a cigarette to smoke, and stopped their questioning for that day.

On another occasion they told him that, as they knew he was not telling them the truth, he was to be placed in a dungeon without food or water, and kept there until he either told the truth or died. Leonard believed this threat would be carried out, and when he returned to his cell, he gave last messages to a friend who was next to him, and asked him to give them to his wife and family. He was not called up for further questioning for five days, and when he was, he asked if this threat was to be carried out. The interrogator replied that it had only been a joke.

During this time all those taken from Changi were in the most appalling cell conditions in the military police head-quarters. The commission already referred to described them as follows:

> The internees were crowded, irrespective of race, sex, or state of health, in small cells or cages. They were so crowded that they could not lie down in comfort. No bedding or covering of any kind were provided, and bright lights were kept burning overhead all night. From eight a.m. to ten p.m. inmates had to sit up straight on the bare floor with their knees

up, and were not allowed to relax or put their hands on the floor, or talk, or move, except to go to the lavatory. Any infractions of the rigid discipline involved a beating by the sentries. There was one pedestal water-closet in each cell or cage, and the water flushing into the pan provided the only water supply for all purposes, including drinking. It should be recorded here that nearly all of the inmates suffered from enteritis or dysentery. No soap, towel, toilet articles or hand-kerchiefs were permitted, and inmates had no clothing other than that they were wearing. The food supplied, normally rice, occasional vegetables, and weak tea with no milk or sugar, was less than half of that supplied by our own prisons' depart-ment as punishment diet for Asiatics . . . The three women taken from Changi prison were detained in exactly the same conditions as the men, and shared cells with male prisoners of all races. They were afforded no privacy, even for their most intimate requirements, and any attempt on the part of Euro-pean men to screen them was broken down by the guards . . . The buildings resounded all day and night with blows, the bellowing of the inquisitors, and the shrieks of the tortured . . . In these conditions, and this atmosphere of terror, these men and women waited, sometimes for months, their summons to interrogation, which might come at any hour of the day or night.

For three weeks after his three days of torture, Leonard was in a semi-conscious state, but as his wounds began to heal and his physical condition improved, his spirit of faith and love rose to meet the suffering and evil of this cell life. His own words, taken from the broadcast sermon already quoted, are the best descrip-tion of this resurrection of faith.

It is true, of course, that there were many dreary and desolate moments, especially in the early morning. I was in a crowded and filthy cell with hardly any power to move because of my wounds, but here again I was helped tremendously by God. There was a tiny window at the back of the cell and through the bars I could hear the song of the Golden Oriole. I could see the glorious red of the Flame of the Forest tree, and something of God's indestructible beauty was conveyed to my tortured mind. Behind the Flame tree I glimpsed the top of Wesley's church, and was so grateful that the Church had preserved so many of Wesley's hymns. One that I said every morning was the first hymn we sang today *Christ Whose Glory Fills the Skies*. Do you remember the second verse?

> Dark and cheerless is the morn
> Unaccompanied by Thee;
> Joyless is the day's return
> Till Thy mercy's beams I see.

And so I went on to pray,

> Visit then this soul of mine
> Pierce the gloom of sin and grief.

And gradually the burden of this world was lifted and I was carried into the presence of God and received from Him the strength and peace which were enough to live by, day by day.

This spirit passed from Leonard to others. A number of those in the cells asked him about the meaning of prayer. It was impossible to talk during the day, but at night, by keeping a careful watch, they were able to talk in whispers. These exchanges grew into a rich fellowship, so that when people were taken out of the cell to the torture rooms, they knew that those behind would be praying for them and sharing in spirit their suffering.

In March 1944, Leonard was moved to a different cell. Here there was a Chinese, who had already been in touch with two Christians in other cells, a Presbyterian called Robert Burns, and a Lancashire man named Sam Travers. They had taught the Chinese a good deal about Christianity, and told him to get in touch with Leonard if he could. Leonard continued to instruct the Chinese at night, and on Maundy Thursday, in the early morning, he was baptised with water from the lavatory basin in the cell. Two further incidents are best described in Leonard's own words:

Every Sunday after February, when I was moved to a less conspicuous cell, I began taking the communion service. On one occasion a most courageous woman, a Christian, who was Mrs. Elizabeth Choy, a mission teacher, and was in because of her help to internees, was sweeping the corridor. She came past our cell and I stopped the service for a moment to tell her what we were doing. A few minutes later she came back and knelt outside the bars and received the Sacrament through the bars. She was not seen by the guards. Our cell was just round the corner, and, if the guards came, we could see a shadow on the wall, so had to keep constant watch. We used a little rice which had been given to us some time ago, and had communion in one kind, and when we got our weak tea for breakfast, we used it as a Loving Cup.

The other incident concerned one of the military police who had taken part in the torturing to which Leonard was subjected. In a letter to Brigadier Sir John Smyth, V.C., written in April 1967, Leonard said:

Before I left Singapore in 1945 I arranged for a Japanese-speaking evangelist from the School of Oriental Studies, Miss Hentie, to come out to Singapore to work amongst the Japanese and to preach the gospel of reconciliation. She had to work amongst what were known as the 'surrendered personnel', and also amongst those who were in prison for war crimes. When I got back in 1946 I found what splendid work she had done, and there were quite large classes going on in preparation for Christian baptism amongst both sets of people.

In 1947 I took various services of baptism and confirmation in the cathedral for those who had been prepared, and I got permission for those who were serving sentences to be marched up from the prison. Among those that I baptised and confirmed was one of the men of the military police who had been responsible, four years earlier, for taking part in my own torturing. I have seldom seen so great a change in a man. He looked gentle and peaceful, even though he was going back to serve a ten-year sentence, and later he received communion at my hands in the prison.

So it was that events indeed turned full circle, and good came out of evil. But this is to anticipate, and we must return to the time when Leonard was sent back by the military police to the internment camp now established at Sime Road. This happened on May 26th, 1944, the internees having been moved from Changi at the beginning of the same month. Leonard went to the hospital attached to the camp, and after some weeks was sufficiently recovered to join his fellow internees. When he left the military police headquarters, he had lost four stone, but he was able to jump down from the lorry unassisted. In the next few weeks he was visited by Hayter, Bennitt and others, and he gave them an account of what had happened in the preceding seven months. Soon after his arrival at Sime Road, he asked for the novel he had been reading when he had been removed on October 17th of the previous year. It was important to him that he remembered the place where he had left off, and was able to start reading again at once.

When Leonard was fit to come out of hospital and return to the camp, he shared quarters with Hayter, Norman Alexander, and A. A. Thompson. Leonard, Hayter and Thompson had been in the same cell at Changi, and when Leonard was taken away by the military police, Alexander had taken his place. Thompson, who had been an accountant in Kuala Lumpur, played an important part in the development of events in Leonard's questioning. He had been responsible for keeping an account of all the monies that Leonard had borrowed and got into the camp both before and after his internment. Thompson was the only person interrogated at Changi on October 10th who was not taken to the military police headquarters. During the time of Leonard's interrogation, one of the Japanese brought to Changi a note from Leonard telling Thompson to provide a list of all loans of money, their sources and amounts. There were about sixteen different entries, and Thompson was able to provide from memory a list which corroborated what Leonard had said under examination.

There was only one sum unaccounted for. This was for ten thousand dollars. The camp bank had received ninety thousand dollars, and at this point they had sent out a message that they did not require further funds; but a hundred thousand dollars had in fact been sent in by the time this message was received, and the extra ten thousand dollars never appeared in the camp bank accounts. A man called John Long, who acted as a lorry driver, had kept this ten thousand dollars, and used it, with the aid of one of the camp doctors, to buy further medical supplies. On his expeditions to the town Long used to make notes of all the shipping he could see in the harbour, and the raid by the military police on Changi took place soon after some British submarine raids on Singapore harbour. The Japanese almost certainly connected these with the spy activities which they thought originated in Changi. At any rate, when it was discovered that the missing ten thousand dollars had been used as described by John Long, the latter was executed, and it was soon after this that Leonard was released to the camp.

In some ways conditions in the open camp at Sime Road were better than those in Changi, but by this time the rations had deteriorated, and most of the inmates were in the third year of their internment. The camp gardens were the only source of vegetables, and the single addition to the small ration of rice. As the tide of war turned against the Japanese, more internees were taken off the gardens and put to work on digging tunnels inside the camp, intended for defence purposes when the allied attack came. Leonard gave an Advent course of sermons on prayer, and shared another course of sermons on the Church in action. These reflected the two strains of thought which were uppermost in his mind; namely, what prayer had come to mean to him and others during their time of interrogation, and the task awaiting the Church in the new situation which would exist when the war was over.

It was still possible to supplement the very inadequate amount of food supplied by the Japanese with purchases made on the black market. Leonard, like some others, was able to cash cheques through intermediaries, and use the money for buying extra food. It is clear that his action in this regard did not escape criticism. As already mentioned, when Leonard, Hayter and Adams were interned they took with them as much in the way of supplies as they could. Amongst these was a considerable amount of tinned food, some of which had been kept in store at Bishopsbourne. Leonard refused to hand over the whole of this to the camp quartermaster, and there was a considerable argument between the two of them as to how much Leonard should hold on to for the use of himself and his immediate companions. This got around the camp, where the inmates had been in poor conditions for over a year, and started Leonard off badly.

Leonard's treatment by the military police and his courage completely restored his reputation. However, something of the same kind happened again during the time at Sime Road. Leonard bought a Red Cross parcel from someone else for £125; he sold his spare episcopal ring on the black market, and he made direct purchases of food through cheques he was able to cash through intermediaries. There was no reason why the internees should not use any resources they could command to improve their situation, but the fact remains that Leonard's attitude in this matter did alienate the opinions of some in the camp. Leonard must have been aware of this, but he did not change the line he took. It seems certain that he felt that there would be a tremendous task ahead when liberation came; that he had an important part to play in this, and he must be as fit as possible to do it. In fact, in the month after he was set free he was able to do the hardest work he had ever done in his life. It was both a strength and weakness of Leonard's character that when he had fixed upon a course of action which he believed to be right, he was not open to any criticism which others made of it. Adverse criticism often had the effect of hardening his attitude, and he would go beyond what others thought reasonable in disregarding it. There was, however, a certain ambiguity here. For, while he regarded it as a weakness to give way to the opinions of others when he had made up his mind, he still often felt that he ought to have their respect, and was put out when he did not get it. He was right and they were wrong, and why couldn't they see it?

Leonard had always taken the attitude that the Church people who had been interned expected to be supported by their fellow churchmen outside who were Asians, and he had no hesitation in using the name of the Anglican Church to borrow money for himself and other internees, both before and after his own internment. Some European inmates of the camp resented this attitude. They also resented the way in which Leonard was one of the first to get out of the camp when the British troops arrived. The formal surrender of the Japanese was signed on August 14th, and soon after that parachutists were dropped to tell prisoners-of-war at Changi and internees at Sime Road that the war was over; but the main body of British troops did not arrive until early in September, and the Japanese maintained discipline in the town until then. .

In a report written some years later, Leonard said, 'We were kept in the camp long after we heard the news of the Japanese surrender, and were not free to go away from the camp until some time in September. I was one of the first out, as I had a house to go to, and was not under authority, such as a Government servant.' This was entirely in character. He was a bishop. There was urgent need to make contact with Asian Christians, who had carried on the work of the Church on their own through the last two and a half years, and to organise relief for the Asian population both in Singapore and in the rest of the diocese. Leonard was their bishop, and just as he had taken it as natural that they should support him when in internment, so now he felt it equally natural that he should give them all his attention, time and care. Internment was over. He had finished with that part of his life; there was an urgent job waiting to be done. It was the Chinese outside who needed him now, not his fellow internees. If this was how he felt, then it was quite in character that when he left the camp he took with him some magazines, papers and chocolate that the chaplain of H.M.S. *Sussex* had brought in the day before. One fellow internee recalled years later, 'I did not mind about the chocolate, but I would have liked to keep some of the papers.' It was not that Leonard was deliberately thoughtless, but just that, like others who have great powers of drive, when the moment of decisive action had arrived, nothing else really came within the focus of his attention.

So it was that Leonard returned to Cathedral House, to find Ah Sing, the Chinese houseboy, who had been with him since Hong Kong days, waiting for him at the door. There followed a month of intensive work, at the end of which Leonard received the following letter from the brigadier who was head of the Singapore division of the British military administration, and chairman of the Emergency Relief Committee:

May I express upon behalf of all my officers and my colleagues on the committee, our great appreciation of all that you have done during the past month to get social welfare and relief measures started off again in Singapore. Your great assistance to me personally in all these matters has been of inestimable value. I have been lost in wonder since my arrival back, that you have had the energy to do all you have done after what you have been through. We wish you a safe return

42

to England, and God speed you back when you have enjoyed the rest you have so richly deserved.

On Sunday, September 23rd, Leonard preached at the official thanksgiving service in St. Andrew's Cathedral, and some extracts from this show his thoughts at the time. He said:

Our thanksgiving is first for the cessation of hostilities. There is a deliverance from battle, murder and from sudden death. Looked at from God's point of view this was a civil war between His children, though so few acknowledge Him. A second cause for thankfulness is that we were found worthy of victory. But to pour out thanks for a favourable verdict runs the risk of seeming to betray a bad conscience and to have a poor idea of the judge's office. Yet we must use our judgment and without priding ourselves too much on the height of our ideals, we have good reason to say that the war was between humanity and inhumanity, and we thank God humanity won.

Then, turning to the other aspect of his theme, service, he went on:

For the most part I am talking to those who are strong. Strong not only as a conquering force but strong in the power you can exercise. Most of you, whatever your rank or station, are by your victories equipped with tremendous power. What are you going to do with it? Upon all of us there still lies a great and heavy responsibility for which we need not only the physical and mental strength, which, in large measure, are already assured, but a spiritual strength for which we are dependent upon God Himself by prayer, recollection and sacraments. This is of vital importance. Many victories have been won without any recourse to spiritual power and there is a great danger that we fall back upon that agelong fallacy that education, discipline, government or scientific machinery will give us all the strength we need to solve the problems of the world. It is a vain thing fondly imagined and may God save us from those years of futile disillusion that so many experienced between two wars . . . Many of the weapons which have been most useful in winning the war must be discarded if we are to win the peace . . . Our greatest need at the moment I think is to take upon ourselves the burden of the infirmities of the weak. In war it is impossible to tolerate the timidity, the conventionality, the feebleness and the prejudice of the weak. Patience with such weakness and futility is impossible in wartime and many of us have lost the art. But now St. Paul's injunction is relevant. You that are strong must bear the infirmities of those who are weak. This patience is needed now, and something more than patience, an understanding sympathy. If we are going to help people we must for their sakes forgo something of our own strength and share the fear, the dimness, the anxiety, and the heart-sinking through which they have to work their way. We will have to forgo the privilege of strength in order to understand the weak and backward, to be with them, to enter into their thoughts, to advance at their pace . . . If we are to serve aright God and our fellowmen we ought not to try and prove to ourselves or others that we are strong. Self-assertion, wilfulness or even standing aloof in critical reserve is not the Christian way of proving our greatness. The kings of the earth exercise dominion and power, but, said Jesus, 'The greatest among you is he that serveth.'

Soon after Leonard got back to the hospital in Sime Road, after his seven and a half months in the military police headquarters, Sorby Adams, who was working in the hospital, asked him what he had learnt from his long ordeal. He answered, 'I have learnt that the purgatory of joy is greater than the purgatory of suffering, because it does not destroy.' He referred to this again in his broadcast sermon in 1946, when he said, 'For months afterwards I felt at peace with the universe although I was still interned and I had to learn the lesson or the discipline of joy. How easy it is to forget God and all His benefits. I had known Him in a deeper way than I could have imagined, but God is to be found in the Resurrection, as well as in the Cross, and it is the Resurrection that has the final word.'

In March 1969, Leonard went back to Singapore to take part in a B.B.C. film. The programme was called *Mission to Hell*. Jean-Paul Sartre has said that, 'Hell is other people.' Possibly the converse is also true, and if this is so, this programme might have been more properly called *Return to Heaven*. For it was then that Leonard felt most certain of his faith, and the living presence of Christ both in his ordeal and after it. He felt accepted and upheld by his fellow prisoners, and knew that he also gave strength to them. This was in complete contrast to the torture of his schooldays. The feeling of fellowship that he came to know in those years at Singapore was a unique experience which remained with him all his life. He knew that the grace of God had transformed hell into something like heaven.

On October 13th, he left for Dunedin on the way to join his wife and family in Australia, whom he had not seen for nearly four years.

CHAPTER 3

Family and Home

THE VILLAGE OF WITTON GILBERT lies some five miles west of the city of Durham. Anyone who, in the years between 1888 and 1892, happened to be passing along the country road which linked the village and the city, would have been likely to meet a solitary figure stepping out briskly. This was John Wilson making his way to or from St. Cuthbert's Society in the University of Durham. He was attending lectures there with the purpose of taking his degree and being ordained into the ministry of the Church of England. In the pursuit of this aim, he covered the ten miles on foot every day in term time for four years. He was ordained deacon in Durham Cathedral in 1892, and became curate of Gateshead Fell, where he stayed for the next nine years. In 1895 he married Mary Adelaide Halliday, and, on November 23rd, 1897, their second child, Leonard John, was born.

Leonard's paternal grandfather, James Wilson, was a schoolteacher. His first post was at a school near Norham, Co. Durham. In 1864 he became the master in charge of the National School, at Witton Gilbert, and he remained in this post for thirty years. In 1894 there was a row between him and the rector, and he resigned. He applied for, and obtained, the position of postmaster at Witton Gilbert, and remained in it until his death in 1911, actually signing the cash account sheet on the last day of his life. He was a strict disciplinarian and a very good teacher. His son, John, went to his father's school at Witton Gilbert and stayed on as a pupil teacher. It was from this background that he launched out on his university studies and his preparation for the ministry.

Leonard's maternal grandfather, Thomas Halliday, was a very different character from James Wilson. He was born in 1846 and died in 1933, and while those eighty-seven years must have brought many anxieties and not a little hardship to his wife and family, there were few of them which he allowed to be dull or monotonous for himself. His son once told Canon Leslie Wilson, one of Leonard's brothers, 'Your grandfather had no idea of the value of money. He would tip the chambermaid a guinea, provided she had a pretty face, and give her a kiss as well.' He was never worried by his debts, which were frequent and sometimes large, and used to say, 'It's a foolish man who worries over his debts; they are the worry of the lender, not the borrower.' He was a man of drive and enterprise. At one time he was in business on Tyneside as a coal-exporter. A Spanish firm, which was one of his chief customers, collapsed, and his business came to an end. Nothing daunted, he set out for Spain, and spent over a year there and in Portugal, becoming fluent in both languages. At the same time he made a deal with the Spanish firm. He arranged for the debt owed him to be repaid in part by a ship-load of sherry, with which he returned in person to Tyneside. His newly acquired knowledge of Spanish and Portuguese enabled him to get the post of secretary to the firm of Armstrong Whitworth. However, he lost his job as a result of his heavy drinking and extravagant living.

In 1868 Thomas Halliday had married Mary Hall, and a year later their first child, Mary Adelaide, was born. After he had to leave Armstrong Whitworth, he decided to explore pastures new. He went with his wife and two sons to join the eldest boy who was in Santa Lucia, U.S.A. The adventure did not prosper, and in 1904 he returned alone to England. Here he stayed with his daughter Adelaide and his son-in-law John Wilson, at Birtley, where John had moved as curate from

Gateshead Fell in 1901. The house in which John and Adelaide lived belonged to Thomas Halliday, and they lived there rent-free in return for keeping him. He stayed with them for four years. He was a gifted raconteur and Leonard remembered the vivid stories his grandfather told as he sat roasting chestnuts by the fire.

In the meanwhile Mary Halliday, with the two sons, Tom and Willie, had moved from Santa Lucia, first to Canada, and then back to the United States to Mound City in Kansas, where she had relations. Thomas rejoined them in 1908. Running true to form, he had such a celebration the night before sailing, with his friends who came to see him off, that he left all his luggage on the quay, and this had to be sent on after him. After his arrival at Mound City, he tried his hand at a number of different jobs, including farming, chicken-rearing and coffee-planting. Here he lived out the rest of his days. His wife died in 1922, and he died of typhoid fever in 1933. In spite of his unstable and sometimes riotous life, Thomas seems to have had a lively religious faith. He wrote simply and directly to his grandchildren in Australia on their religious duties. A typical passage appears in a letter to a granddaughter written in 1918, 'May God grant that the Prince of Evil may be banished and chained to his den, as we are given to hope in Holy Scripture. Do you rely on Him and seek His guidance in all your actions, and be assured that He will keep you and never desert you.'

It was while he was curate at Gateshead Fell that John Wilson married Mary Adelaide Halliday. She had been educated at Gateshead High School. She was always keen on the arts, and in her late teens ran away from home with the intention of going on the stage. This seems to have been an adventure in the spirit of her father, but Thomas did not approve and fetched her home in some anger. John Wilson was thirty-three and Adelaide Halliday twenty-six when they were married. Their first child, Edith, was born in 1896, and Leonard the following year.

John Wilson, like his father, was a stern disciplinarian. His ten-mile daily walk from Witton Gilbert to Durham was regarded by him as a natural and necessary part of his plan to get his degree and be ordained, and typified his attitude to life. Once he had made up his mind on a course of action, he would stick to it, whatever the obstacles. With this determination went a great power of concentration. He was endowed with a retentive memory, and a splendid speaking voice. He combined a strict, puritan view of life with a strong liberal political outlook. As far as his religious opinions were concerned, he was an evangelical, though never a fundamentalist. In later life, he was influenced by Leonard's more liberal views, and on one occasion Leonard, who had come under Streeter's influence at Oxford, took his father to hear and meet Streeter when the latter had come to Newcastle to lecture. He also persuaded him to read some of H. E. Fosdick's books. Leonard's mother had a less rigorous attitude to life than her husband, and if Leonard's love of poetry and the romantic side of his character were inherited, it was from her that he derived them. For part of the time that John Wilson was curate of Birtley, Adelaide ran a private school there. She was a woman with an attractive personality which won attention and respect from those who met her. As a cousin of the family once remarked to Leslie Wilson, 'When Adelaide entered the room, all conversation stopped, and everything seemed to centre on her.'

It was during the years at Birtley that the younger children were born; Oswald in 1901, Bernard in 1906 and Leslie in 1909. Mary Adelaide died soon after Leslie was born. With a growing family, and no financial resources beyond John Wilson's salary as curate, and what his wife was able to make from her private school, there was no money for extras in the Wilson home. The children were often dressed from bundles of used clothes which had been given to the household. Their only holidays were in vicarages, mostly in County Durham, where John Wilson acted as *locum tenens*. Oswald died at the age of three. Leonard, four years his senior, was devoted to him, and this tragedy made its mark on the boy of seven. It was a foretaste of a loss, similar but much deeper, when many years later his much beloved eldest child, Christopher, died at the same age.

Leonard's early relationships with his mother were not as strong as those with his father. He used to say that he felt he had been born too soon after his sister Edith. For his father Leonard always felt admiration. As a boy his natural affection was tempered with respect. John Wilson was very strict with himself, and he was strict with his children. In later years, when Leonard was grown up and independent, there was a strong mutual affection and friendship between father and son, which lasted until the father died in 1945. It was typical of this later period that when Leonard was invited to become bishop of Singapore, it was his father's opinion that he was very suitable and should accept which delighted him as much as anything else.

Family life meant a great deal to Leonard. As has already been related, when he was beaten and tortured by the Japanese military police, he said he saw these men as they had once been, 'As little children playing with their brothers and sisters and happy in their parents' love.' In many men such language would have been unreal and extravagant, and there may have been those, who, hearing the Singapore story, thought they were extravagant in him. But this was not so. For Leonard they were completely true. The idea of the closely united, happy family was immensely important to him, and like most deeply felt ideas, was a strange mixture of realism and romanticism. The roots of this feeling about the family, which remained with him all his life, were buried deep in his own childhood, and both aspects of it owed much to the home in which he grew up, and to the ties which bound him to his parents and his younger brothers.

CHAPTER 4

Early Years: School – The Army – Knutsford – Oxford – Persia – Coventry

MODERN PSYCHOLOGY HAS CLAIMED that it is the earliest years of infancy which are the decisive factor in the formation of the individual's attitude to life. The evidence for this comes from the consulting rooms of psychiatrists, and for those who have had no cause to resort to psychiatric treatment the experience of these very early years remains hidden beyond consciousness. The reaction of people to their schooldays may be less important, but it is something of which the individual is fully aware. There are those who look back on their time at school as one of the happiest times of their life. Leonard Wilson was emphatically not one of these. He hated his years at school, where he suffered to the full all the pains and agonies which a bad boarding school is able to inflict on those who do not fit into its system. That the only permanent marks on Leonard of this dreary time were positive rather than negative is, perhaps, evidence of the truth in the point of view of modern psychology. Leonard's upbringing in a home which, however poor, was a place of love and understanding, was proof against the years at school where, so far as he was concerned, both these things were absent.

Leonard had begun his schooling at the Gateshead School for Girls, and after a short time went to Newcastle Grammar

School. This was not a success, and in the autumn of 1908, when he was ten, he went as a boarder to St. John's, Leatherhead, a school founded for, 'Sons of the poor clergy of the Church of England'. Mr. Richard Millard, who was a contemporary of Leonard's at St. John's, recalls, 'We were all poor, but I think Wilson was exceptionally so.' He went back to school with nightshirts, as the family purse could not afford to buy pyjamas, and wearing the leather boots of his village home. In the kingdom of the blind, the one-eyed man is king, and Leonard's school-mates, like many others before and since, were quick to make play with such things. After lights were out in the dormitory, Leonard was made to get out of bed and do a whirling dance which would reveal the nakedness of his four foot one inch frame. On one occasion, when he had provoked a concerted attack, he was held down and his hair was completely fixed with a bottle of liquid gum.

It was not only the boys who ganged up against Leonard. He was a butt of several of the masters. School reports are notoriously ill-informed documents, but four years of Leonard's reports make consistent, if very depressing, reading. The very first, for the term ending Christmas 1908, sets a pattern, which, with slight variations, remained constant throughout the four years. His work during the early part of the term was distinctly unsatisfactory. His writing was bad, owing entirely to indifference. His name had been entered in the Black Book, and he had been caned twice, once for lateness and once for 'dissembling'.

Mr. Jack Easterling, another contemporary of Leonard's at St. John's, recalls:

He was not much of a scholar or athlete. The only distinction I can remember was that he was a treble soloist in the choir. Discipline was very rigorous, and he always had the knack of getting into trouble. He told me a few years ago that if, while at school, he had had to assess the chances of himself and his contemporaries becoming bishops, honesty would have made him put himself at the bottom of the list. We should all have agreed with him.

While it is true that had Leonard been met with more human understanding by those in authority, his schooldays would have been very different, it is also true that the school was not entirely to blame. Richard Millard writes, 'Any old Johnian, contemporary with Bishop Wilson as a boy at the school, will confirm that he was unpopular and disliked generally. It is difficult to explain or even really know why. He was too clever; there was something about him that "got under your skin".'

In later years, Leonard was never one to take adverse criticism lying down. He had a gift of repartee which often took his critics by surprise, and sometimes had an edge to it which made them uncomfortable. Such a gift, unless exercised with restraint and an eye to the occasion, does not endear a schoolboy to his fellows or to his masters. Leonard may well have fallen foul of both because he was not one to speak or act with caution when provoked. However, the fact remains that the authorities at St. John's failed completely to recognise any good qualities in Leonard, and showed no attempt to understand the reasons for his failure to co-operate. On his return to school after the holidays in which his mother died, Leonard was told off by one of the masters for standing and gazing unhappily out of the window. He said, by way of explanation, that his mother had died during the holidays. To this the master replied, 'What do you expect me to do about that, Wilson? Weep?' It is not surprising that when Millard, who helped Leonard over the appeal for the Singapore diocese after the war, asked him how he compared his time at school with his days in internment, Leonard replied that St. John's was the worse of the two.

When Leonard returned to England from Singapore, and there had been much publicity in the Press about his imprisonment and torture, he had a letter from E. A. Downes, who had been his headmaster for most of the time he was at St. John's, in which Downes said, 'Are you the Wilson whom I used to beat at school?' Leonard replied that he was, and that Leatherhead had been a good preparation for the Japanese prison. Downes replied on a postcard, 'I'm glad we had our uses.' Another story of this rapprochement comes from Easterling who recalls, 'When Wilson returned to England after his imprisonment, Dean Downes, who must have been about the last of the flogging headmasters, said, "Now Wilson, what are we going to drink? Beaune, I think; you can't beat Beaune." Wilson's comment was, "Can't you? It must be about the only thing you haven't beaten." Downes took it very well and laughed heartily.' If the old man was running true to form, so was Leonard.

It was typical of Leonard, and perhaps one of the fruits of his Singapore experiences, that when he was back in England, he renewed his connection with St. John's, Leatherhead. When he was in Birmingham he had a visit from Millard, who told Leonard how interested he was to hear that he had been doing things in connection with St. John's. He told Millard very simply that he had been tempted not to go back to the place, but that he had come to the conclusion that it would be unworthy not to do so. Indeed, up to the time of his death, he continued to interest himself in St. John's. He did in fact often visit the school and preach there, and he was generally present at the annual school dinner in London. 'One Sunday,' writes Easterling, 'when he celebrated Holy Communion in the school chapel during the Old Johnian Cricket Week, one of his contemporaries, not I think much of a church-goer, told me that Wilson had made the service mean more to him than it had ever meant before.'

This last recollection and comment on the way in which Leonard took the Holy Communion service is one that is shared by many others who knew him. Norman Jarrett, who was with Leonard in Changi, writes, 'One of the most impressive of his traits was his wonderful way of celebrating Holy Communion.

54

Every word in the service was made to tell, and every time he celebrated, the familiar words seemed to take on a new meaning or new nuances. His voice held you and humbled you and helped to bring you into the presence of God.' And John Hayter writes, 'There always seemed, in the way in which he said them, to be particular significance for him in the words of the consecration prayer, "In the same night that he was betrayed." '

In 1915 Leonard made an attempt to join the army, but this failed as he was discovered to be under age, and the fact that he was still very small did not help his attempted deception. However, in May of the following year, he joined the training battalion of the Durham Light Infantry. He told a friend years later that when he went into the army he thought how kind the sergeants were. They spent a lot of time swearing at him, but not one of them clouted him or gave him a beating, and he found this a pleasant contrast to the way he had been treated at school. He did in fact enjoy his time in the army. He was soon made a sergeant, and was later commissioned to the 13th Battalion The Bantams, and served with them in France towards the end of the war.

Leonard had an interesting reunion with the regiment in 1939, when he was Dean of Hong Kong. He was taking the Christmas Day service for the 1st Battalion. An officer of the regiment, who knew Leonard, relates how he was standing next to a sergeant who had at one time been the forward hooker in the County Durham rugger team. As the dean arrived, the sergeant exclaimed, 'Why! He was in the sergeants' mess last night wearing a regimental tie; we didn't know he was the dean.'

Shortly after the 1914 war, Leonard attended a reunion at St. John's, Leatherhead. Richard Millard remembers how Leonard buttonholed him, and in the course of conversation told him that he hoped to go up to Oxford and be ordained. 'But,' said Leonard, in a way Millard never forgot, 'I am going to be the new kind of parson, not the sort of thing you and I know about.' Millard thought at the time that surely the Church would never accept anyone like Wilson for Holy Orders.

However, by 1919, Leonard was at Knutsford where he came under the influence of F. R. Barry and Mervyn Haigh. Knutsford was a unique experiment in the life of the Church of England. In his life of Mervyn Haigh, Bishop Barry writes of it:

> We were led to new understandings of the Christian faith and its possibilities, and of the meaning and mission of the Church, such as had not been given to any of us before, so that some of us were converted to a new outlook, wider than any of those sectional loyalties which at the time counted for so much, and (God be praised) count for so much less today. And that they do count for so much less (I speak as a fool) is partly due to Knutsford.

The leadership and fellowship which Leonard found at Knutsford certainly helped him to see more clearly what the aims and ideals of 'the new kind of parson', of which he had talked to Millard, ought to be. He entered into the activities of the place with zest, and made two lifelong friends, J. P. P. Gorton and W. F. (Jock) Malcolm. Canon Peeke who was a contemporary at Knutsford writes:

> The three friends were very different. Gorton was something of a mystic, deep thinking, not very articulate, a man of deep piety. Malcolm was a man of great humour and fun. Wilson too enjoyed fun. They took part in the May Day parade. The Knutsford May Queen procession is celebrated in the Cheshire and Manchester area. The students at the gaol joined in the fun, dressing up in all kinds of humorous costumes. I think it may have been these three that instigated the fun. They played a big part in the 'general election' campaign for various committees, and the writing of various posters. Tubby (his substantial build was evident even then, for he was at once known as Tubby Wilson) was a good mixer, liked fun and games, and was indeed popular with his fellow

students. His outstanding characteristics were, to me, a sensitive social conscience, impatience with tradition which had outlived its usefulness, and, what was thought of then as a modernist theological outlook.

From Knutsford Leonard went up to Queen's, Oxford, and took the shortened course, as did so many who had spent some years in the army. Among his contemporaries at Oxford were Robert Stopford, now Bishop of London, Max Dunlop, Harold Mulliner, Oliver Fielding Clarke, Eric Featherstone, and Kenneth Parsons. Some of these were at Hertford, and Leonard seems to have had more friends there than in his own college. One common interest was the Student Christian Movement; another was a close association with Streeter, who was then a dominant personality among students who were connected with the S.C.M. Robert Stopford recalls how a party of them, including Leonard, would go to Streeter's room in the evening for long arguments and discussions. Streeter would sit by his fire, apparently asleep. At 11.20 p.m. he would come to life, sum up the whole discussion, and send them all off at 11.50 p.m. Certainly Leonard greatly admired Streeter, and his growing theological understanding owed much to him. Life at Oxford came as a revelation to Leonard. Like others who have found their schooldays intolerable Oxford gave him a liberation of mind and spirit. He made friendships, some of which lasted a lifetime, and those who were closest to him, though sometimes irritated by his inability to answer letters, never forgot his friendship.

In October 1922, Leonard left England to join the staff of Stuart Memorial College, Isfahan. In May of the following year he resigned and left Persia, travelling overland to Cairo. He returned to England and, in October, went to Wycliffe Hall to prepare for ordination. The exact course of events is difficult to trace. It is clear there was a row in Persia, but, at this distance of time, when most of those involved are dead, it is not possible to be definite as to the reasons for it. Some hints of these, and of

Leonard's feelings, appear in letters he received during this period from his friend Eric Featherstone. Featherstone had left Oxford earlier than Leonard and was working in Nigeria. Writing from there in June 1922 he headed the letter, 'My seventh and your second' and underlined the words heavily. He wrote:

Dear Len,

I have heard from Broadbent that you stroked the Togger 1st Eight (on account of which honour many congrats.) and therefore I know you were alive at that time, but whether some mischance has befallen you since then I know not. At any rate I have not had a letter from you since heaven knows when, and my patience is about exhausted . . . What the devil is the matter with you? Are you just slack (at letter-writing), or have I mortally offended you? I am driven to some such thought. Two letters in sixteen months, and in those you said how you missed me at Queen's, etc., etc., etc., well why not write and relieve your feelings??!!

After more to the same effect, he added a postscript, 'Don't flee the wrath to come by running off to Persia, before I get back, or any other similarly futile place.'

Featherstone was home on leave in August, and must have seen Leonard then. On December 24th he wrote from Carlisle:

My dear Len,

Delighted to receive your letter of November 17th written on a tanker . . . Well, I hope you have long ago arrived safely at Isfahan, and there find numerous good folk, who are making you feel thoroughly at home . . . I was in Oxford for the first weekend in December, and for ten days later in London.

He went on to describe a party of Queen's men in Piccadilly Circus on the night of the university rugger match, and how they had been moved on by a bobby, and added:

I wished you had been there, Tubby. I feel it is almost too

58

bad telling you all about it. However, when you come back, and I am at home, we will celebrate.

There is then a gap in Featherstone's letters until June 24th, when he wrote from Nigeria:

Dear Len,

Without the slightest doubt, your letter dated April 14th and just received, is the most vague and unsatisfactory I have ever received from you.

You have been in your blessed (?) Isfahan months and have received letters from me, and then you write a letter in which I am to 'forgive the brevity and lack of wit'. I cannot forgive the brevity, because it is quite a long epistle (albeit of little news) and the lack of wit *would* have been forgivable if the letter had been otherwise interesting and informative . . . After your one and a half page tirade against the bishop and archdeacon, the only bit of downright writing in the letter, I think I probably agree with the bishop. Why shouldn't he disagree with your modernist views? I imagine he dislikes you more because of them, than because you happen to like his wife! But of course you always did fancy yourself with the ladies!

If he tries to get rid of a heretic according to his lights as a C.M.S. man, well, he's only doing his job. Mind, I don't say you *are* a heretic, but I gather you modernists and Anglo-Catholics like to think yourselves as such; and incidentally nobody has any manner of right to disagree with you. If they do you are all up on your hind legs at once . . . Yes, you've known me six years, but I wonder whose fault it would have been if the connection had broken down.

What do you mean about stroking a 'Cats' boat? Are you returning to Oxford? How will you do that if you have another job handy, whatever that may be? Possibly you have been offered a directorship in the Anglo-Persian Oil Company? Who can tell from your letter?

Well, you say you are 'rather lonely'. As a matter of fact I guess you are darned fed up with the whole show, and if so, I am jolly sorry this letter won't buck you up much, but you've really got to have it. When I recognised your writing on the envelope I was jolly bucked and keen to hear how it fared with you, but what an unsatisfactory feeling at the end.

Leonard does not seem to have answered this letter until October 23rd, when he was settled at Wycliffe Hall. Featherstone received it a month later and answered the same day:

My dear Len,

I don't regret my letter, but I do regret that it reached you when it did. You must admit that if it had arrived while you were still in Persia before your misfortunes came about, you would have treated it much more lightly.

You say to me, 'You are not convinced that the bishop acted dishonestly.' Fortunately I have kept the letter you wrote from Isfahan, which provoked my outburst, and I have re-read it. You forget that that letter gave me no idea of the seriousness of the position, or that it was likely to have the effects upon you which it seems to have had. You wrote almost gaily of the bishop firing you, but not getting you out of Persia as you had other work in view. No mention at all of his 'dishonesty', so that there seems to be some reason why I shouldn't be convinced of it!

Can't you see that after the friendship that grew up between us I had a right to expect a letter from you before this one, dated October, telling me you had left Persia, and not be left to hear the news third and fourth hand via a C.M.S. magazine and my people at home? If I'm of any value to you, have you never any desire to write and let off steam at me except when you are in a position to tell me 'Everything in the garden is lovely'? A friend can take the bitter with the sweet, and have a shot at being sympathetic, even though he be a cynical one. I'm sorry but I simply can't understand your silence after you got home from Persia.

Perhaps it was as well that I wrote as I did in June, and that you received it when you did, because it stirred you up to answer, and give me some idea of what you have been through. It's only because I now realise this that I can swallow your letter. You would not have written as you do, if you were not in a pretty bad way.

It is evident that the events in Persia created a strained relationship between Leonard and his family. Featherstone, who was a friend of the whole family referred to this in the same letter.

I am most sorry about what you say about your separation from the home folk; it's an awkward thing for me to enter upon, but is the fault all on their side? From what I have seen of them all I can't think it. For God's sake have a try at reconciliation, or you may regret it later on, not for your own sake only. Tubby, I'm dead serious about it, and don't go off the deep end and tell me that *of course* I can't take your side a bit. And for heaven's sake don't say you appear to cause unhappiness to those you care for most; if you imagine you do, have a jolly good think, and see if you aren't possibly to blame.

This long letter had more than a Pauline ring about its ending. Featherstone said:

Write and tell me that you are bucking up again, and then I can write you a really cheery letter. If you don't I shall start spending money on cables, so that for very shame you will write. If you aren't bucking up, write all the same, though I can't promise I'll take another letter like the last so mildly. I would probably leave on urgent private affairs.

This letter clearly evoked a grateful and friendly reply from Leonard, written while he was home at Gateshead for Christmas.

61

In February Featherstone wrote:

My dear Len,

After your letter of December 27th your previous epistle of unhappy memory has been torn into little pieces and consigned to the flames in my cook-house. So *that's that*.

I note your desire to spend some time with me when I come home, *before* your ordination: presumably you either want one good spree to tide you over your first months of ordination, or else I am not to be regarded as fit company for a young ordinand. Thanks! Then in the next para. you tell me of your 'gorgeous rowing binge'; and your prowess as a 'wriggling' scrum half. Presumably everybody was so tight that they each saw several Tubbies and always grabbed the wrong one. I hope you hadn't a degree to take the next morning!

Whatever the reasons for the row in Persia and Leonard's resignation, it is clear that these had no effect on his relationship with church authorities at home. He was accepted at Wycliffe Hall, with the support of the Bishop of Durham, who secured a grant for him from the diocese. He was in touch with C.M.S. headquarters, and the Reverend H. S. B. Holland, who worked there, was making inquiries to see if Leonard would go to him as a curate. Very soon after this, the Bishop of Coventry was supporting Holland's request with enthusiasm. Holland wrote:

My dear Tubby,

I cannot call you anything else as that is the way I always speak about you. Do you remember that when we had that talk here on your return from Persia I said there was no knowing but in a year's time I might have a living and be ready for a deacon? Curiously enough this has happened, and I am going off to be sub-dean and vicar of the cathedral at Coventry next April. It looks to me as if I might very likely need a man sometime next year. I write now to ask if you would really be willing to consider coming to me as a deacon. I can say nothing definite yet of course, as I am not in the job, but I don't want anyone else to get in before me with you. When do you hope to be ordained? Is it Advent 1924? I shall be very glad to hear from you, and to know that service with me would not be altogether inacceptable to you if the way opened out.

Leonard must have answered enthusiastically, as a week later Holland wrote again.

My dear Tubby,
    Your letter was a great delight to me. Of course you will have to consult the Bishop of Durham and get clear about your obligation to him and his diocese. With regard to the point about my not being certain whether I shall be wanting anyone by next autumn, I can only tell you when I mentioned the matter to the Bishop of Coventry, his immediate reply was, 'Book him, book him', so I don't think there will be much doubt on that score.

The matter must have been settled within a short time, and Leonard worked at Wycliffe for the Oxford ordination course. The Bishop of Coventry arranged a special Michaelmas ordination for which he had secured one other deacon. Leonard was anxious to avoid the gap between the end of the summer term and Michaelmas, and suggested to Holland in April that he might come to him in July, if the bishop would ordain him at Trinity. He wanted to be doing a practical job, and he would have no grant once he had left Wycliffe. Holland replied that it was impossible to make a change then. He had only just arrived in Coventry himself, and did not feel he could go to the church-wardens for an extra quarter's salary, and he could not ask the man whom Leonard was to replace to leave before September. He also thought the bishop would be annoyed, as he had gone to the trouble to make this special arrangement for the ordination in September. He suggested various things with which Leonard could fill part of the time, and which would help financially. One of these was that he should go as a helper to the Student Christian Movement for their summer camps. This, in fact, Leonard did, and evidently with success, as he received a letter of rapturous thanks from A. G. (Poggee) Pite. At length, after having written an essay for the bishop, which was thought remarkably good, he was duly ordained in Coventry Cathedral in September.

For the next three years Leonard worked with great energy and success at Coventry. For the first time he was in a position where he could exercise to the full his pastoral gifts. He formed a very lively fellowship of young people. In 1967, Leonard and Mary were guests of honour at a dinner attended by about sixty people, of whom forty were former members of this fellowship founded forty years before. One of the founder members of this group, Mr. Mervyn Miles, writes:

> He led us in all the usual pursuits: camps, outings, dances, tennis parties, fêtes, and many of us remember the breakfasts after early morning communion, and the services held in the slums and poor courts round the cathedral, which we attended out of loyalty to 'our' Tubby. He loved life, and some were shocked by his unorthodox behaviour as a parson, and a cathedral parson at that. But for a majority of people he opened a new door to the Church and religion . . . The present provost, Dr. H. C. N. Williams, thinks that such an association as ours, inspired by loyalty to a young curate over forty years ago, must be unique . . . We were proud of the Bishop of Singapore, but it was the young curate we remembered and held in such affection.

Leonard had a great gift with people. Again and again, throughout his life, the story is the same. His concern for individual men and women, and the time and trouble he would take to understand them, and share their needs, was a dominant trait in his character. He was greatly loved by all sorts of people, because his heart went out to them in spontaneous interest, kindness and affection. The first time a young ordinand met Leonard was during the general strike of 1926. He went from Oxford to Coventry to enlist the support of the clergy on behalf of the Archbishop of Canterbury's efforts to bring about a settlement. He was met by Leonard who put him up for the night in the chapter house where Leonard lived with other members of the cathedral staff. At this distance of time he does not remember what went on at the meeting held to discuss the crisis, but he has a very clear recollection of Leonard's personal kindness, which made him feel at home and was a source of strength in a situation in which he knew nobody, and was not very sure what he was supposed to be doing. Many years later the same man preached for Leonard in Manchester Cathedral. He still remembers very clearly how, when Leonard conducted him to the pulpit, and made his formal bow, he whispered, 'God be with you', and how much that informal blessing meant to him before he preached. It was in ways like these that Leonard endeared himself to his many friends.

On return from a holiday in September 1925, Holland wrote to Leonard:

My dear Tubby,

Your presence would have been much nicer than a letter to greet me, but I am jolly glad for your sake that you are out of the whirl for a bit. You may think you aren't much of an organiser; but I should like to see the man who could do more creative work in his first year of Orders than you have done. I just thank God for all you have done for Him, and there's a big bit of personal gratitude for all you have been to me, dear man.

About your requests:

1. By all means go and spread yourself on S.P.G. at Kenilworth. You were always more typical of them than of C.M.S.!

2. Just to keep you loyal to C.M.S., I shall let you go to

the Y.P.O. conference on October 7th, and will even pay your fare out of my fund.

One of Leonard's few surviving letters gives a picture of some of the things he felt at the time. It was written to his aunt at Witton Gilbert.

Dear Auntie May,

It has been a long wait until I could find the time to write a decent letter to you and even now it may not be good. I suffer from that rather bad failing of not doing things because they aren't my best. I rather wait until I can do my best which of course cannot come unless I practise. I really have been very busy; it is always late when I get to bed and the memory of work left undone is very paralysing. On the whole I am extremely happy in the lots of various jobs I have to do. I still have such a very very long way to go before I achieve the sort of regulated Christian life which has to come if our work is to be of any use.

But this letter is first of all to thank you for your lovely present of tobacco. Thank you so very much. I think after trying many others it is the kind I like best. Thank you too for your letter and the good wishes from all of you. My birthday was a busy day to me being Sunday, but I enjoyed it all the same. So much of the kind of work I have to do is office work and I have a very bad business head. However a volunteer secretary comes in three evenings a week and types a great many of the business letters which have to be done each day. I wish I could get quicker to these jobs. However that will come by practice . . .

Part of my work is secretary to missionary societies and I have had to do a lot of preaching and lantern lectures. I have been to Stratford-on-Avon and to places in and around Rugby. Sales of work and socials need a tremendous amount of organisation. The hundred of little details keep me very

66

busy . . . But it's all very good for me and I can see it leading the way to happiness.

Here's my love to you all and so many thanks for your presents. Yours affectionately, Len.

Towards the end of 1926, Leonard was beginning to feel unsettled. News of this reached Max Dunlop, who was then serving as a deacon at Southport, through a mutual friend, Harold Mulliner. And in January, Dunlop wrote a long letter in the course of which he said:

I gathered you meant, definitely, to leave Coventry in June this year: and Harold passed on to me an echo of what I had heard from you before, that you half thought of abandoning Orders at the same time. About Coventry I have interest, but little concern: you will then have been two years or so there, and a shift might be advantageous from more than one point of view. But about the other, I have considerable concern, if only that of the fox who lost his brush; I should strongly object to you regaining yours.

What is the matter? . . . Harold said something about the Sudan Civil: but if you irk under your superior in the Church (the bishop), because he is otiose on the question of the Virgin Birth, you will surely irk as much under a superior in the Service who is otiose on the question of illegitimate births of half-castes, and so on. Perhaps you feel that generally you are unsuited to the Church, i.e. that the ideals you serve cannot, by you, be effectively served in the Church. If this is the case I do sympathise with your difficulty. For myself, as you probably know, I am simply giving the thing a trial, and regard deacon's Orders as in no way irrevocable, nor priest's Orders either, of course. But in this last and important aspect of the desire to abandon Orders, i.e. one's own effectiveness in carrying out one's own ideals within the Kirk; while certainly a man is the ultimate judge of himself, he is also a thoroughly incompetent one. When I look at you and your work, in the frankest light I can bring to bear, I am convinced that you are, taken as a whole, extremely effective in working for the ideals I suppose you to have.

After more in the same strain he ends:

To sum up this paragraph with sweeping Pauline magnificence; if you leave the Church, I shall think you a damned fool.

Whatever Leonard's feelings were at this time, they were resolved by the prospect of new work. The chance of becoming Principal of the Old Cairo Boys' School had come his way, and by the spring of 1927 he was fully embarked on plans to this end. This enterprise, which he started with such high hopes, ended in disaster. The story is fully documented. It is a good example of ecclesiastical politics. This will not be of great interest for those who care for none of these things, but Leonard regarded the controversy as important. He had all the relevant letters copied and bound into a single volume, and they do throw light on some aspects of his complex character.

CHAPTER 5

Egypt and the Church
Missionary Society

LEONARD WAS ACCEPTED BY the Church Missionary Society in
April 1927. He had said that he expected to be able to leave
Coventry in June. In fact he did not leave until August, because
Holland was taken ill, and Leonard stayed on to tide over
the time of Holland's absence. He was at home in Gateshead
for a few months, and actually reached Cairo in February
1928.

During this period there was an exchange of views between
various people concerned as to how Leonard should play himself into the job. When the matter had first been mooted by
Leonard, he had agreed to serve under the Reverend A. J. Toop,
the principal of the Old Cairo Boys' School, for one year, and
then take over from him. The C.M.S. authorities in Cairo, the
Egypt Mission standing committee, had a meeting in April
1927, when they expressed the view that it would be better for
Leonard to take two years rather than one before assuming the
principalship. They felt that two years was needed to acquire
the kind of facility in Arabic which they regarded as essential for
anyone holding that post. There was a fixed course at the School
of Oriental Studies, and the four examinations in Arabic which
would be expected, could not be passed under two years. If,
however, this suggestion was not acceptable, they did not wish to
make it an absolute condition, and would comply with the

original terms, as they were anxious not to lose Leonard for the Egypt Mission and the Old Cairo Boys' School.

In view of what happened later, it is interesting to note that there were two different opinions about the best course for Leonard to follow. While the majority of the C.M.S. people working in Egypt were so strongly insistent on the importance of learning the language, Geoffrey Lunt thought otherwise. Eighteen months later, when the row was in full swing, he made this clear in a letter to Leonard. He had fought on the Egypt committee to let Leonard go straight out as principal of the Old Boys' School, and learn his Arabic gradually as he went along. He thought it would be a great mistake for him to be hanging about in Cairo for two years, with no definite job except preparing for Arabic examinations, while C.M.S. folk could sit down and make comparisons between him and the principal who was still there.

Events proved how right Lunt was in his judgment. Had his advice been followed, there might well have been no row, and Leonard might have made a success of the school. Professionals are often jealous of the amateur who takes over a position of authority where they consider professional expertise is of the first importance. They are nearly always wrong; for what the job needs as a first priority is a man of conviction, who knows what he wants done, and has the necessary power of leadership to achieve it. Had Leonard been put in the post for which he had been appointed at once, he might well have found his feet then and not have had to wait to find them until Singapore. He might have launched the Old Cairo Boys' School into becoming another Trinity College, Kandy, which was the hope of those who really understood the educational possibilities in Egypt at the time.

It is worth recalling that Alek Fraser, who had made Trinity College, Kandy, what it was, and went on to create Achimota in the Gold Coast, never learnt a language in Ceylon or Africa.

Leonard accepted the suggestion of the Egypt Committee,

and, after the delay already referred to, arrived in Cairo in the second week of February 1928. He was there until May 1929. Nothing of special significance happened in the first eight months. At the beginning of November the committee had before it a report on Leonard's work. Leonard had applied, and been accepted, for a post as lecturer in the Coptic Theological Seminary in Cairo. However, the acting patriarch had vetoed the appointment, and then Leonard had accepted a post in the Coptic Secondary School. The committee questioned the wisdom of his undertaking work which involved twenty teaching periods a week in the school and four in the seminary, when it was necessary for him to acquire a considerable knowledge of Arabic before taking over the boys' school. Leonard replied that he needed the experience the Coptic school would give him; that it would be worthwhile trying to influence boys, some of whom might be going on to the seminary later; that there was a possibility that the objection to his lecturing in the seminary might be overcome, and that he intended to take the first two language examinations in March. The committee agreed, with some reluctance, to Leonard going on as suggested for a trial period.

Although there is no direct evidence, it seems reasonable to infer, in the light of later events, that there were two factors, not mentioned, lying behind the committee's attitude. First, Leonard was dissatisfied with the work which he was able to do, outside the study of the language. He was helping at the cathedral, preaching there and elsewhere, and getting to know the British community in Cairo. It is clear that he was a very popular person in these circles, but they were not the C.M.S. circles. There were some in the C.M.S. world who did not approve, or were jealous of, the way in which the principal designate was spending his preparatory time. Leonard must have been aware of this. It is doubtful if he did anything to conciliate those who were critical; that was not his nature. Moreover, he was in a difficult position. His only reason for coming to Egypt was to do a particular job as principal of the boys' school, and he was being kept hanging about, filling in time in jobs, many of which were not directly related to his future. However, he realised how important for his ideas for the future of the boys' school the goodwill of the British community was. In his view it may have seemed as important as the support of C.M.S. circles. His application to the Coptic authorities reflected his feeling that he wanted to be getting on in a practical way with the work ahead.

The other question that arises out of the deliberations of the Egypt committee is why the acting patriarch vetoed Leonard's appointment as lecturer at the Coptic Theological Seminary. The committee evidently thought it would have been a good one both from the point of view of C.M.S. policy, and for its general usefulness. It would appear that the answer must be that rumours of Leonard's views, expressed in the pulpit in Cairo Cathedral and elsewhere had reached the patriarch.

After the committee meeting, Leonard wrote to Toop, who had been at the meeting. He suggested that Toop should remain in charge for another year, and that he, Leonard, might be able to help with the physical training work in the school. Toop replied that he had consulted with some of his fellow missionaries and come to the conclusion that he would prefer to keep to the original plan and leave at the end of the current academical year. He added that the drill master was doing fairly well, they were only paying him a small sum a month, and he did not think he would need to avail himself of Leonard's offer. It is obvious from the tone of the letter that there was not an easy relationship between Toop and Leonard.

At the end of January, the Reverend W. Wilson Cash, general secretary of the C.M.S., passed through Cairo. Complaints were made to him about sermons preached by Leonard in the cathedral. Cash saw him, and had 'a personal and quite frank talk' about the matter. Before going any further with Cash, Leonard consulted Max Dunlop, who was then working in a parish in Alexandria. Dunlop had been there some nine months, and during that time he and Leonard, who were old friends, must have seen each other frequently. A letter from Dunlop dated February 6th, throws some light on how the underground situation was developing. He wrote:

Dear Tubby,

May I now teach you to suck eggs? It seems you are in a complicated position in Cairo, and this doctrinal stand of yours makes a clear view of the position in your own mind essential, and essential too a view of your objective. As what do you preach? As free-lance parson, or as C.M.S. head-elect? If you are still as uncertain of the headship as when I saw you last, then you preach just now as free-lance. In my opinion not much is to be gained by that sort of preaching; the task we have is to change a society from within. And further, though free-lance in spirit, you are officially and nominally C.M.S. Your doings then reflect on C.M.S. But unless one is heart and soul in a society one has no right to oppose it, unless it is doing positive harm. If you have determined to take on the headship, if you are as much C.M.S. as Cash or any of them, then strength to your elbow . . . My last relative thought at the moment is that there is always the chaplaincy staff. Into this you could go now if uncertain of the headship to the point of carelessness about it; or, into which you might be allowed to retire if the C.M.S. kick you out. If you are to fight as C.M.S., then the most important point is to refuse to retire gracefully, but to force them to put you out, if things should come to such a pass, which I hope sincerely they will not.

A month later, Leonard wrote to Cash:

Dear Mr. Cash,

Your 'conversations', like those of 'Melines', are very disquieting. I mean those you had with me about my views and those you subsequently had with Morrison on the same subject. I gathered from him merely this, that you were distinctly worried. I am sorry, for you have many infinitely larger issues to which you must needs give much attention . . . No one can do good preparation work with the Sword of Damocles hanging over his head. A certain measure of security is essential. I know you cannot promise me a safe lodging here and peace at the last, but you can tell me whether I shall have your support in these troublous times.

Leonard went on to point out that he had no wish to waken doubts in those secure in their traditional beliefs, but he felt called to help those honest doubters who did not see that there was an anchorage for faith independent of biblical or ecclesiastical authority. He had been speaking to people who had asked him to deal with some of these theological questions, and he thought he had kept within the limits set by the C.M.S. He went on, 'I do believe in the divinity of Christ. On the manner of that divinity I thought that many of us were agnostics these days, and I did not scruple to say so.' He concluded by saying he was anxious to serve the C.M.S.; that his views had not changed since he was interviewed by the executive in London, but it was very difficult for him to make plans for the future without the support of Cash and the Egypt committee.

In his reply Cash enclosed a copy of the statement formulated by the C.M.S. in 1922 to define the position of the society, and pointed out that this was a pledge to its supporters that it would only take on those who could subscribe to the resolution. He went on, 'It seems to me that within the concordat of C.M.S. are a body of men who do quite definitely accept the Virgin Birth, and the inspiration of Scripture. They do not demand a definition of inspiration, verbal or otherwise, but the references in the resolution are perfectly clear that they do regard Holy Scripture as a supreme authority.' He then pointed out that this seemed to clash with what Leonard had said in his sermon, and with things said in their conversation, and asked Leonard to go through the resolution and let him know whether he accepted the position of the society as set forth in it.

On March 29th Leonard replied to Cash, repeating that he thought his theological views fell within the limits of the C.M.S. resolution, but this resolution, being in general terms, could be interpreted in different ways and was in fact so interpreted by members of C.M.S. He did not feel that Cash's interpretation was the only one, and therefore he must give his. He wrote, 'I do "fervently acknowledge the Lord Jesus Christ to be my Lord and my God", but I do not accept the Virgin Birth. I do regard Holy Scripture as "a supreme authority", but the meaning of Holy Scripture has been and is being revealed to me by the mind of the Church and the guidance of scholars.'

Leonard showed this letter to the Reverend S. A. Morrison, a member of the C.M.S. Egypt committee, and asked his opinion of it. Morrison said he thought that he might have put down his views at greater length, and at Leonard's suggestion wrote a letter to Cash which was agreed between them. As Morrison's letter was central to the content of the theological side of the ensuing controversy, the relevant passages must be quoted in full. He wrote:

The central question is, to my mind, one of Christology. If I understand Wilson aright, he does not believe in the pre-existence of Jesus before the time of his birth at Bethlehem, except in so far as all persons and things, prior to their existence in time, have an existence in the eternal purpose and will of God, and that in Jesus there is revealed the supreme and eternal purpose of the Father.

Furthermore, he would not be prepared to state, as a dogma, that there is any difference in kind between the divinity of Jesus and that of other men, but that it is a difference of degree only. He believes that while God is revealed in scientific truth and beauty, Christ truly and perfectly reveals the character of God, in so far as this can be revealed in

75

human life, but that we all do so, in so far as we partake of the spirit of God, which Christ partook of perfectly. We, too, are Sons of God potentially, as Christ is actually.

By this time Leonard was depressed and disturbed, and asked Cash to cable a reply. But C.M.S. at home was disturbed too, and hearing the first faint rolling of distant thunder, Cash got in touch with Holland and one or two others who were liberally inclined members of the executive committee. In May he wrote to Leonard to say he had not replied earlier because he wished to talk things over with Holland and others. He had now come to the conclusion that no further useful purpose could be served by correspondence, and it would be fairer to the C.M.S. and to Leonard if the whole matter could be discussed in person. Leonard would be coming to England in June and the sooner they met the better. At the same time he made it clear that the ramparts were being manned. He wrote:

I do not think, however, that you should interpret this [the suggested face-to-face discussion] as necessarily meaning that you will be able to return to Egypt, and I would like to make it perfectly clear that in postponing discussion until your return, I am not prejudicing any action the society may consider it necessary to take, after further interviews with you. They may of course decide that you should return to Egypt; but on the other hand it is equally possible, and some think probable, that they may decide that you cannot return to the mission.

The fact that Cash agreed to postpone action and meet Leonard was mainly due to Holland. Holland was, of course, deeply involved. Apart from the fact that he had a great love and respect for Leonard as an intimate friend, he had helped him into the C.M.S. opportunity of the Old Cairo Boys' School. In addition he had centred all the work done in Coventry Cathedral round the World Call on Leonard, as 'their' missionary. On April 18th, he wrote to Leonard:

My dear old Tubby,

It's just a week since I saw Cash and had my first news of your problem. I had no idea till then that it had come to a head . . . Things do seem pretty serious; Cash evidently won't face a heresy hunt, but I have since written to him, before I got your letter this morning, begging him to postpone action till we can all see you and talk it out in the summer.

After saying that none of Leonard's statements seemed to him outside the C.M.S. position, and if they were, thousands of other people like himself were outside it too, he said that he himself had always been cautious about his public statements, and he went on:

And I suppose that leads me to the one thing I could wish had not happened, and that is your public expression of theological opinion. I was so longing that you would get well into the saddle and get everyone's confidence before you got on to controversial things especially Christology. But I'm not fault-finding, for I never want you to be anyone but yourself, for it's yourself I love, and I know it is asking for the impossible to keep you muzzled up . . . Of course here there would be an appalling difficulty; wrongly or rightly we have so built up our missionary interest and our response to the World Call round your work and personality that the loss of you to C.M.S. would make things frightfully difficult. But it must be faced and a way through found.

In April, Leonard had taken the first part of his Arabic examinations and failed them. He was unwell at the time, and very much worried about the controversy that had arisen and his own future position. However, it did not help his case. Writing in May to invite Leonard to Coventry directly he got to England, Holland admitted to being worried about it, 'It was rotten luck and I am not at all surprised at your going down under the circumstances. But it will tell against you.'

By the end of May Leonard had arrived home, seen F. R. Barry, then at St. Mary's, Oxford, and left the revelant correspondence with him. Writing to Leonard the day after his visit, Barry dealt briskly with the points raised in Morrison's letter, saying that anyone who proposed to make statements 'as a dogma' on such questions as the pre-existence of Jesus, or 'the outworn dilemma of degree or kind', would merely show a total failure to appreciate the issues involved. He wrote:

> Nobody who has thought or read at all could possibly lay down the law in this way on points no human being can understand in any case, and about which there is no available evidence. And further, speaking as an examining chaplain to three bishops, I should gravely suspect any man who did so, and should probably report to the bishop that the candidate had not begun to think.

He pointed out that in any future statement Leonard made to C.M.S., he should amplify what he had said in his letter of March 29th about the Virgin Birth to make it clear that what Leonard meant was that, having regard to the admittedly uncertain evidence, he was not prepared to dogmatise about it; not that he necessarily regarded it as untrue. Barry went on to say that he did not think there was anything in Leonard's position which was not covered by the Archbishop of York (Temple) on the one hand, or Canon Streeter on the other. He ended by saying:

> If, as you assure me, the question between yourself and the C.M.S. lies solely on the theological issues which are disclosed in this dossier, then I should say quite definitely that if you are asked to resign on these grounds, the C.M.S. will make it quite impossible for even moderate liberals to support them. It is not a question of what is called modernism, but of such

elementary recognition of the great issues raised in theology as ought to be required, as a condition of ordination, from any candidate for the Ministry.

A week later Barry wrote again, having in the interval met Cash at a conference at High Leigh. Reporting this meeting, he said that Cash had agreed with him that Leonard's views were consistent with being a minister of the Church of England, but the C.M.S. stood for something, and if further questions were raised in their committee, as they were bound to be, he would not be able to justify himself and there would be a demand for blood. Cash had said that the C.M.S. was very unhappy about the whole thing, but if Leonard were to return to Egypt, the situation might become worse. Barry went on to say that in his view the happiest solution would be if Gwynne, the Bishop in Egypt, would offer Leonard a chaplaincy of the ordinary kind, so that he could go back to work amongst the British community. In any case, after what had happened, it was not likely that he would be happy in C.M.S. circles in Egypt. Barry concluded by saying he had written to Gwynne to ask him if he would do this.

Shortly after this, Max Dunlop, now back in England, had his first news from Leonard of what was going on. From this time until his return to Egypt at the end of September, Dunlop spent much time and thought on the issues involved. He was as dedicated to the cause of liberalism as Leonard, and more clear-sighted than Leonard about the feelings and motives of those in the opposite camp. He saw Barry at the end of the second week in June, in order to clear up some points that had arisen from the various meetings of the previous weeks. He told Barry that Leonard was very disturbed at the chaplaincy suggestion, and he would not touch it. All Leonard wanted was the job at the Old Cairo Boys' School. Barry accepted this.

During May and June two things happened which had an important effect on the controversy. The first was that Leonard had a meeting at Salisbury Square, with Mr. Cash, Mr. Hooper, the Africa secretary, and Mr. Harris, the editorial secretary, at which there was a full informal discussion of Leonard's views. They all three felt that these were not within what was commonly regarded as the C.M.S. position. Hooper was very anxious to keep Leonard, and he wrote an informal note to him on June 22nd to say so, adding that he believed Leonard had great gifts to give the Christian Church in Egypt. At the same time he made it clear that he thought Leonard was claiming more individual freedom than was permissible to anyone who accepted membership in the C.M.S. He wrote, 'In my view, membership in the Society does involve a voluntary surrender of liberty beyond certain limits; and when those restrictions become intolerable, a member can withdraw, but I don't think he is entitled to ask that the limits shall be subject to individual adjustment.'

The other development was that it became known to those involved in the dispute that the complaints from Egypt involved something more than theological questions, and Bishop Gwynne was aware of these other matters. These complaints included the charge that Leonard had antagonised people in Egypt by his general attitude and done more to split the Mission than to unite it.

Directly Leonard heard of this he wrote a number of letters. He wrote to Dr. Lasbrey, to Mr. Toop, and to Dr. W. S. Hunt, a friend of his, who was a doctor working in the Old Cairo Hospital. To Mr. Toop he made the point that, though he had not seen as much of him as he would have liked during the last year, when they had met they had always been on friendly terms, and he asked for an assurance that Toop would welcome him as his successor. In his reply, Toop said:

With regard to the special point you raise in your letter, my own policy in all matters that concern our Mission is to cut out all personal prejudices, whether good or bad, and to welcome wholeheartedly as a colleague anyone and everyone sent to us by Salisbury Square. Therefore, if you return to Egypt, you may certainly count on my doing what I can to help or advise in regard to the school, and the corporate life of the Mission.

To Dr. Lasbrey Leonard wrote saying that one or two people were trying to burke the doctrinal issue and seeking to get rid of him on the grounds of character and work, and he wanted Dr. Lasbrey's assurance with regard to the sermons he had preached; that he had consulted with Dr. Lasbrey before taking on work in the Coptic school; and that he had asked him what the attitude of C.M.S. would be if he asked permission to become engaged to be married. Dr. Lasbrey replied that he had heard Leonard preach on a number of occasions in St. Mary's Cathedral in Cairo, and he had always found his sermons profitable and helpful, and had told others so. He knew that one of Leonard's sermons had been criticised, and there had been a good deal of talk about it. He had been away in Khartoum and had not heard that particular sermon. He saw nothing to criticise in the sermons he had heard. As to teaching in the Coptic school, Dr. Lasbrey confirmed that Leonard had consulted him, and then referred to the meeting of the Egypt committee of November 6th. As to matrimonial engagement, Dr. Lasbrey confirmed that Leonard had asked him about this, and said that his recollection was that he had told him the usual C.M.S. rule was that three years in the field and the passing of language examinations should precede marriage, but that in the case of senior men, and this would apply to anyone taking over the Old Cairo Boys' School, there might be a relaxation of the rules. He then added:

Referring to what you say about getting to know the British community, etc., I sometimes rather wished you were living in C.M.S. circles, as one felt you were a bit cut off, but at the same time I knew it to be Lunt's opinion, as well as that of some others, that it would pay to get in touch with English Cairenes and hence your residence at the clergy house.

In response to Leonard's request, Dr. Hunt wrote as follows to Holland:

I have just heard from the Reverend J. L. Wilson that it is being said that he has been antagonising people in Egypt by his *character* and that he has done more to split the Mission there than to unite them. Having known Mr. Wilson during his eighteen months or so in Egypt, and having seen a good deal of him in that time, I would like to state that in my opinion his character and personality have done a great deal toward interesting English people out there in the work being done by the C.M.S., and everybody I've met with, with whom I have ever discussed Mr. Wilson, whether they agreed completely with his views or not, at any rate had a great regard for his personality and for himself as a man.

On July 6th Bishop Gwynne wrote to Leonard:

My dear Wilson,

I am afraid this letter is going to hurt you badly. I am very sorry, but I feel sure that it is kinder to tell you quite plainly, that for the present it is not possible for you to return to this diocese. Looking at the whole situation, your inability to pass your Arabic examinations and allowing yourself to be side-tracked from the job you came to do, have alienated you from the missionary workers in this part of the diocese. And from what I gather your return to this diocese as a chaplain would create difficulties. I should like to see you at work under such a man as Geoffrey Lunt for a few years. For your own sake I know it would be unwise for you to work here. I am, yours ever, Llewellyn Gwynne.

Leonard wrote to the bishop asking for an explanation of his letter. He contested Gwynne's statement about his relationship with his fellow missionaries in Egypt, and asserted that all the plans he had made and the work he attempted were done with the future of the boys' school in mind. He told the bishop that he was sending a copy of the bishop's letter and his reply to Mr. Hooper at C.M.S. headquarters. In his covering letter to Hooper he asked for the opportunity to clear away the alienation charge, so as to leave isolated the question of doctrine which had to be settled separately.

At the beginning of August, Bishop Gwynne wrote from Scotland, where he was on holiday, saying he could not see Leonard before the third week in September when he would be in London, and ended, 'I have nothing more to add to the letter I wrote at the beginning of July.'

At the end of August, Max Dunlop, who had been brought up to date by Leonard, took the initiative and wrote very fully to Leonard, Holland and Barry, and enclosed the draft of a letter he proposed Leonard should write to Gwynne. Dunlop's object was to secure that the two issues of character and doctrine should not be confused. It was the second that mattered, but the first must be cleared away so as to leave the second free of irrelevancies. In his letters to Holland and Barry, he urged them to exercise all the pressure they could to make Gwynne amplify his charges, which he had refused to do, or withdraw them. In the course of his letter to Barry he wrote:

I understand from Tubby that Gwynne actually suggests that Salisbury Square are putting up a false case in fixing on Tubby's doctrine. As if that harassed office, with the B.C.M.S. muttering behind it, and the Liberal–Evangelicals prowling around, would deliberately choose to make a doctrinal case of what was really a character one! The truth is it might well welcome the character charge as a way out from the doctrinal difficulty. But if the character case can be cleared, then Gwynne's judgment that there is no serious doctrinal difference between Wilson and the Egyptian C.M.S. (which is the truth generally speaking), may be useful when negotiations at last get on to this, the real issue.

On August 29th, Leonard wrote to Bishop Gwynne, following the draft which Dunlop had sent, as follows:

Dear Bishop Gwynne,

Your letter of August 3rd seems final, but I venture to ask you to reconsider it.

I came home this year to discuss with C.M.S. doctrinal differences which it had been suggested were between us. I felt, and after some discussion I still feel, confident that what differences there may be are not essential, and that I can regard myself as a loyal member of the Society within which I am to try to realise my dreams of Christian education in Egypt, and it is my hope that the Society can find me acceptable.

You have raised another issue. Your letter of July 6th says, in effect, that I am unfit for the special work of the Cairo school, and adds that neither could you employ me on the chaplaincy staff. This is tantamount to saying that as a clergyman I am inefficient, and I am confirmed in my inference that this is what you mean, by your suggestion that I should work for some years under some able clergyman such as Mr. Lunt, who would instruct me. Further, you consider this issue of my character and efficiency as a clergyman to be so grave that you have been forced to raise it whilst the doctrinal question between myself and C.M.S. was still *sub judice*, although you must know that your raising of it rules out discussion of my doctrine by C.M.S. as beside the point. It is, therefore, despite the finality of your last letter, that I venture again to ask what are the actual reasons in your mind against me for the course you have taken.

You tell me they are, first, my failure to pass my Arabic examinations; but, though I know this is much, you are well aware of the circumstances in which I partially failed here: my ill-health, and the many other duties I undertook in my first year, some in direct pursuit of my work for the school, but many of a diocesan character, and above all the distraction which the doctrinal differences of the last few months brought about. Secondly, you say I have alienated the missionaries in Egypt from myself and from my work for the school, but I have received since I arrived home letters from nearly every type of missionary in Egypt, in which they hope that C.M.S. may find room within itself for my interpretation of doctrine, though often the missionaries themselves disagree with my interpretation, in order that I may be retained for my work in the Cairo school, about which they write too kindly. What then am I to make of your personal attitude? I can only think that you were grossly misinformed about me, though by whom I find it hard to imagine, between my leaving Egypt and your letter of July 6th.

Will you not give me an opportunity of personally clearing myself to you, by informing me of the precise charges you have against me?

I have had, of course, to tell C.M.S. in general terms, since I was aware of nothing definite, of your attitude, but I am most loathe that Salisbury Square, or any third party, should come to sit in judgment between you and me about my character and efficiency. I would infinitely prefer that first you would allow me to attempt to satisfy you on that score myself, giving me the opportunity of clearing myself of any particular charge or charges you have against me, and the chance to demonstrate to you that I have not alienated the missionaries in Egypt, but that I have in some measure won their enthusiasm for my plans and methods.

I ask for nothing better than that you should not spare me your suspicion. I should welcome such frankness as a chance of reassuring you of myself, both as my bishop and on personal grounds.

On September 9th, Bishop Gwynne replied:

My dear Wilson,

The C.M.S. brought you out to Egypt. I had nothing to do with your appointment, nor have I ever been asked to give my views on the situation which has arisen between you and the C.M.S. I ventured to suggest how you, a young clergyman, might be helped to more useful service in our Church, as, in case the C.M.S. did not employ you in Egypt, I did not think it wise to offer you chaplaincy work. That is all, as far as I am concerned. I am, yours sincerely, Llewellyn Gwynne.

The bishop left England to return to Egypt in the middle of October, without seeing either Leonard or any of those who were trying to help him. Gwynne had accepted an invitation from Barry to stay with him in Oxford in order to talk things over, but cancelled his visit the day he was due to go.

In the meantime Leonard tried to get matters clearer by another direct approach to Cash. He called twice at Salisbury Square, when Cash was not free to see him, and Cash then wrote to him saying he did not think there was any point in reopening the discussion which had taken place in May when Mr. Hooper and Mr. Harris had also been present. He reiterated his opinion that when the question came before the committee at their September meeting, the decision would be that Leonard could not continue as a member of C.M.S.

Leonard sent this letter to Holland who wrote at once to Canon Storr, who was also a member of the C.M.S. executive committee, soliciting his help. Storr then saw Harris, and as a result of what Harris told him wrote a private letter to Holland, saying he did not think there was anything to be done, and it would be better to let the matter drop. Harris had told Storr that the question was not just one of liberalism in theology, but that there was a general feeling that Leonard was not the right person for work in Moslem lands. Leonard had not made himself *persona grata* with a variety of people working in Egypt from the bishop downwards.

Holland was not put off by this, but wrote a strong letter to Cash to say that Leonard must be allowed a chance of knowing and answering the charges that had been made against him, and he suggested that Leonard should be in attendance when the executive committee met. This had its effect, and Cash invited Leonard to be present at Salisbury House on the day of the meeting in case the committee wished to see him. After the meeting of the executive committee, which apparently did not ask to see Leonard, Holland wrote to give him an account of what had happened. His opinion was that the executive would turn him down. The theological issue and the character issue had become hopelessly confused, and liberal opinion on the executive would not be able to make a case against the general adverse atmosphere which had been created by Gwynne and other church leaders in Egypt. Holland said that he intended to have a long talk with Guy Rogers in Birmingham, but was not hopeful. He went on, 'It is only my knowledge of the executive, not any lack of conviction as to the rightness of our cause, that makes me feel sure they will turn you down.'

Holland saw Guy Rogers three days later, and at once reported to Leonard. Rogers had agreed that it was no good fighting the case any more in the executive. Members of the committee had voted against the secretaries out of thoughtfulness for Leonard, to give him a chance of resigning, instead of being retired. Rogers felt that there was no question of refuting Gwynne's charges because no charges had been made. It was simply a question of atmosphere and the decision of the people in Egypt that they did not want Leonard. This confirmed Holland in his view that it was in Leonard's own best interests not to fight the issue any more but to resign.

Holland's stand in the executive had prevented a final decision being made then, and Cash again took up by letter the question of Leonard's doctrinal position. He asked for a fuller statement on the issues that had already been raised: the pre-existence of our Lord; the Virgin Birth; in what sense Christ was the Saviour of the world; and the nature of the divinity of Jesus. He added that he thought the ultimate result would be as he had previously stated, Leonard's retirement from C.M.S. Leonard did not attempt a further written formulation of his views, but made a last attempt to get the C.M.S. on its part to state in writing which of his views could not be endorsed by the Society. On November 4th, Cash replied that he could speak only for himself and his fellow secretaries, who had advised Leonard, after long discussion, to resign. He could not speak for the committee, who had refused to make any pronouncement until they had had a full statement from Leonard. He recalled that at the meeting in May between the secretaries and Leonard, the issues discussed had been those already raised by his letters from Egypt: the pre-existence of our Lord; the difference between Christ and other men, and the Virgin Birth. He concluded by saying,

Two factors governed the advice we gave you:

1. The fact that you have been working in a Mohammedan country where many Mohammedans would accept most of the points of Christian doctrine as you appear to present them, and where the apparent weakening of the truth expressed in the Trinitarian teaching of the Church would seem to us fatal to Mohammedan evangelism.

2. The fact that you were working alongside of an eastern Church with which the Society has had long associations, and has in the past been able to render to it very great service. The Coptic Church stands with fanatical strength upon such a matter as the Virgin Birth.

It was therefore not with any desire to trip you, or condemn you, or to blame you for your own views (which you have every right to hold in your own way and express as you wish) that we gave you our advice; but simply that the views that gather around your Christology do not seem to us to be compatible with the position taken up by the society which is pledged to an 'evangelical interpretation of the formularies of the Church of England'. It was on these grounds that we recommended your resignation.

On November 15th Leonard replied:

You sum up the views which gather round my Christology as being incompatible with the position taken up by the Society.

The Church at home is comprehensive and includes easily within its compass the views which I hold about the Person of our Lord.

The impact of the Church through its missionary work abroad is sectional and incomplete, as some of the elements which contribute to the richness of the corporate life at home are not offered to the world at large. In other words, the work of the C.M.S. at least is narrower in many ways than the Church at home. Until the distant prospect of the Missionary Council becoming the true executive is reached, existing societies should surely draw away from their sectional basis to the more representative comprehensiveness of the Anglican belief.

To secure some measure of this had been my hope from within, as a member of the Society, but it has become abundantly clear that this course is not open to me at present.

May I assure you again that my hopes and ideals for the Church abroad are true and sincere, for I am convinced that either my hopes will be fulfilled in time, or else the Church of England with all its blessing of wide vision and comprehensiveness at home, will have mingled a curse of narrow views and sectionalism abroad.

Having regard therefore to the interpretation of the Society given me by the secretaries who advised me, I must stand outside the Society and ask you to lay this letter of resignation before the committee.

The C.M.S. accepted his resignation and a month later on December 31st Leonard fired his last shot across Gwynne's bow with the following letter.

Dear Bishop Gwynne,

Perhaps this letter will hurt you but most probably it won't, as you have an admirable way of avoiding anything that hurts. I think I had better tell you quite frankly that in the recent unfortunate controversy between myself and C.M.S., you entered in with many statements which were not only not true, but were maliciously untrue. It is distressing to say the least of it to find that a man who professed such friendship (perhaps that is too strong a word, you wouldn't be capable of such an offence as that) should turn out to be the most treacherous enemy.

Sir, you are as ignorant of the sense of fair play as you are of theology, and your handling of my case was as foolish as it was disgusting.

May I wish you a cleaner mind and ability to learn the truth. J. L. Wilson

As is often the case in controversies of this kind, there were in the end no winners. Church societies, representing a particular Christian emphasis, cannot afford to alienate their supporters by including among their workers those to whom this emphasis is of secondary importance. There may often be, as there were in this case, some on the governing body who take a wider view, but in the day of battle their voices will not prevail against the closed ranks of the faithful.

Leonard genuinely believed that he was called to offer for the C.M.S. post, and he also thought his theological views were a true expression of the Christian faith and compatible with work under C.M.S. Had he played himself in with the kind of caution which Holland hoped he would show, the result might have been different. But that kind of caution was never part of Leonard's character. Gwynne may well have been forced into a difficult situation by the action of some in influential church circles in Egypt, but it does seem strange that he allowed such a complete breakdown of communication between himself and Leonard.

CHAPTER 6

The North of England and Hong Kong

WHEN HOLLAND HAD COME to the conclusion that nothing more could be gained by continuing the controversy with C.M.S., and that to do so would be against Leonard's own best interests, he wrote to Hensley Henson, the Bishop of Durham. Henson wrote at once to Leonard. In his letter dated October 4th, 1929, from Auckland Castle, Bishop Auckland, he said:

Dear Leonard,

I hear from Archdeacon Holland that you are in some kind of difficulty. If you care to do so I should be glad if you could come here next week (I am at home until Saturday, the 12th, when I go to Nottingham) and have some talk. You may stay a few days if you like. Let me know what day you can come. Affectionately yours, Herbert Dunelm.

At the same time he wrote to Holland:

My dear Archdeacon,

I have a considerable regard for young Wilson, and shall willingly do anything in my power to assist him. I have written to invite him to come here, and talk over his plans. What with Modern Churchmen, on the one hand, and these fundamentalist fanatics on the other, the *via media* of reasonable faith is not easy.

It has always puzzled me that respectable Evangelicals,

who are never tired of emphasising the spiritual as against the institutional factors in Christianity, should yet be able to reconcile it to their conscience and understanding both to purchase advowsons and to defend the proceeding. This conduct is not only in itself obviously wrong: but, in its inevitable implication, a clear proof that they have not real belief in the Divine Support, for which they so confidently pray. But when we enter the precincts of the 'religious world', we pass into the sphere of paradox and make-believe. Believe me, yours sincerely, Herbert Dunelm.

Soon after this Henson secured for Leonard a post as curate at St. Margaret's, Durham, where he was to act as curate in charge of St. John's, Neville Cross. Thus began the eight years Leonard spent in parishes in the North.

Leonard does not seem to have kept Holland informed about the result of his meeting with Henson, as Holland wrote to him on November 2nd,

My dear old Tubby,

This isn't a letter, just a line to ask you to write and tell me what you are doing up in Durham; I have only the vaguest idea; is it a daughter church of S. Margaret's? I do want to know; and how you like it. And will you see Tristam?

And do remember that I'd take you on as curate or vicar or bishop any old day; it has worried me stiff that in trying to show you the realities of the situation you have imagined that I have lost confidence. I thought you knew better, dear Tubby. I'm just the same, only sometimes hot and bothered. Thine, Bertie.

There comes a moment in most controversies where more is gained by the participants agreeing to differ and recognising that the truth is not served by an over-obstinate pursuit of the rightness of one's own point of view. There were times when Leonard went on too long thinking that his was the only right attitude, and that those who did not recognise it were either cowards or fools. He had an itch to be right and to feel that others recognised that it was so. This could alienate those in a different camp, and cause unhappiness to the friends in his own. However hardly he had been treated by Bishop Gwynne, his last letter to the bishop was a sign of weakness rather than strength, and Holland's gentle rebuke shows how his determination to vindicate himself prevented him seeing that he was being less than generous to a very close friend who had stood by him in his troubles. This is a paradoxical trait in the character of a man who was universally respected for his thought and care for individuals, for whom he went to endless trouble when they were in any kind of personal need.

In the autumn of 1929 Leonard had become engaged to be married. He had first met his future wife, Mary Phillips, when he was in Cairo. She had been secretary to the American Vice-Consul, but after his death, she worked as a temporary secretary to Bishop Gwynne. When Leonard left Cairo they were not engaged, and during the summer Mary was offered a post on the embassy staff in Athens. At this point she telegraphed to Leonard, 'Do you want to marry me?' He telegraphed back, 'Yes'. Holland knew of the engagement at the end of August and it was formally announced in October. Professor Vaughan Jeffreys, who was a contemporary of Leonard's at Oxford, and became a close friend in later years when they were together first in Newcastle, and later in Birmingham, remembers Leonard telling him that, when he became engaged to Mary, he was a little worried, because he didn't feel swept off his feet as he believed was customary in such circumstances. Jeffreys tried to comfort him with the words, 'You're not likely to have a burst tyre when you've had a slow puncture for years.'

Jeffreys was a lecturer in education at Armstrong College, Newcastle, when Leonard came to Neville Cross, and Leonard decided to do a year's teacher training course at the college. He took a very full share in the life of the university. He was a good deal older than most of the students, but this made no difference to the easy relationships he was always able to make in a social setting of this kind. He coached the women's four of Armstrong College and did some rowing himself. Jeffreys recalls that he was, as always, an enormous success with the girls, and 'hearts broke like eggs'. As a young man, while Leonard enjoyed a romantic feeling towards women, his greatest friends were always men. As he matured he exercised an influence on both men and women, young and old, but it was frequently remarked that he seemed to have a special pastoral gift towards men.

Leonard and Mary were married on July 22nd, 1930, by Barry in St. Mary's, Oxford. For a time they made their home with Leonard's father and stepmother at his father's vicarage at St. Edmund's, Gateshead, until later in the same year he was appointed vicar of Eighton Banks. It was here there began Leonard's close association with William Greer, later Bishop of Manchester, and R. O. Hall, later Bishop of Hong Kong. R. O. Hall was vicar of St. Luke's, Newcastle, and Greer was one of his curates. Hall had a great appeal to young men, and it was round him that there grew up the group which came to be known as the Town Moor Parsons. Hall brought together a number of clergy working in the district, in order that they might meet regularly to discuss their common problems. They met on Saturday mornings at St. Luke's, where, after early communion, they had breakfast together in St. Luke's church hall, and then went on to their discussion until midday.

It was the time of the depression, and the North was badly hit by unemployment. They all felt that this was the gravest practical problem they had to face in their parishes. Sometimes the discussion was doctrinal, and among the books which they studied were Macmurray's *Freedom in the Modern World*, and Reinhold Niebuhr's *Moral Man and Immoral Society*. Leonard was rather shocked by the latter, as he thought it was anti-liberal. During Newcastle race week they took a tent on the Town Moor, where they sold books, and held meetings outside the tent. They were supported by a number of laymen and students. Leonard took a leading part in these meetings and was one of the most winning of the preachers. He had a very good voice for it; he felt that he was reaching people outside the churches, and he was at his best in this kind of setting. At this time in his life he took a pleasure in being very unparsonical, and he never joined any of the local Christian societies. As we have seen, Leonard was determined to do all he could to make sense of Christianity to those who cared about it, but found themselves questioning some of the doctrines which seemed to them a stumbling block to faith. One Saturday night, which was Easter Eve, Leonard rang up Hall from Eighton Banks and said, 'I've got to preach tomorrow; I know the church will be full. What really happened at Easter? I don't want to deceive them.'

When Leonard arrived at Eighton Banks, the church was practically empty.

There was a church school, and he regarded this as an important part of his work. The parish was in the centre of the depression with its unemployment, and he made it his business to try to get alongside the families who were suffering from this. He was on friendly terms with a number of Communists.

One Sunday evening Sir John Priestman was in the congregation at St. Luke's when Greer was preaching. Sir John was a keen churchman and a great sermon taster. After the service he came up to Greer and said to him, 'I want you to come to Roker.' Sir John was the patron of St. Andrew's, Roker, in Sunderland. Greer replied that he could not, as he was booked to go as General Secretary of the Student Christian Movement. He told Sir John to go along to St. Thomas's the next Sunday to listen to Leonard, who was preaching there for the Harvest Festival. Sir John went, fell for Leonard, and offered him the living of Roker. This was in 1935. Two years earlier than this Leonard had been approached by R. O. Hall, who had just gone out to Hong Kong as bishop, to join him there. Leonard consulted Henson, who wrote to him as follows, on September 6th, 1933:

1968   British Legion Festival of Remembrance,
Albert Hall

1916 Private in the Durham Light Infantry

1936 With his father, the Rev. John Wilson, and his two brothers. Left to right: Leslie, Bernard, Leonard

1945   In New Zealand after internment

1945   Giving the funeral address in Singapore for prisoners-of-war who died immediately after the Japanese surrender

1968   At Butlin's, Skegness, with Diocesan Youth Group

March 1949   Dean of Manchester with the family

1960   On the occasion of the visit of Princess Margaret to Birmingham

As seen at the Festival of Remembrance by millions of television viewers

January 1968 In the study at Bishop's Croft, Birmingham, on the first announcement of Leonard's approaching retirement

(*Birmingham Post*)

1963 Christmas Day Epilogue

My dear Leonard,

I shall be pleased to see you on Friday, September 8th, either for lunch at one p.m. or for tea at four p.m.

But it is fair to say at once that I should find it very difficult to persuade myself that it *can* be your duty to leave your work in England, where you have shown a measure of capacity which authorises confidence in your career, and to return to the East, where (in spite of the enthusiastic optimism of the Bishop of Hong Kong) the future cannot but be uncertain and speculative. Moreover, the key to our whole religious policy is industrial England, and to leave work *there* is a grave step.

Add, by way of personal discount, that I don't want to lose you. Affectionately your bishop, Herbert Dunelm.

The Wilsons' first child, Christopher John, was born at Eighton Banks on June 20th, 1931. He was a lovely child and Leonard was devoted to him. He died of meningitis shortly before his third birthday on April 14th, 1934, and ten days later their second child, Susan Mary, was born. A few weeks later, Leonard received the following letter from Bishop Gwynne, from Bishop's House, Cairo, dated May 22nd, 1934:

My dear Wilson,

Job has told me of the loss of your little boy and the great sorrow of your missus and yourself. I write to express my sympathy in your great sorrow. You may not be pleased at any sympathy from me, because of the bitterness you had in your heart against me. Any wrong that I really committed of which I am conscious or unconscious, I hope you will forgive. Your name is still on the list of those for whom I pray. I felt prompted to write you this letter.

Life is too short, and our shortcomings too many for us to judge each other. Whatever you may think, when Job told me of your great sorrow, something much more than regret rose in my heart for you and your missus. I am, yours sincerely, Llewellyn Gwynne.

Unfortunately it has not been possible to trace how Leonard replied to this letter.

John Hayter recalls that when they were in internment together in Singapore ten years later, Leonard often spoke to him about Christopher. He talked of him on the one hand, and of Mary and the other children on the other, in such a way that he seemed to be much nearer to Christopher, and that this was so because there was such a difference between the nature of the barriers. There were times when he felt very close to Christopher. There was one occasion when Leonard and Hayter had been at a gramophone concert at a lovely spot on the edge of the Sime Road camp. The light was just going with a glorious sunset as the music finished, and Leonard told Hayter afterwards that he had at that moment a very strong sense of the nearness of Christopher.

The Wilsons were at Roker for three years, and it was here that their third child, Timothy, was born on March 31st, 1936. In spite of Henson's feeling that Leonard would make his mark in the North, the wish to go overseas must have remained in the background during these years, and when in 1938, Hall invited him to go out to Hong Kong as dean of the cathedral, Leonard accepted. No doubt his friendship and admiration for Hall were strong factors in his decision. Shortly after his arrival there he said to Hall, 'I want to be quite honest with you. I have no particular vocation to come here, but I don't want you to kill yourself.' Those words were to have a meaning that neither of them imagined when they were spoken.

When Leonard arrived in Hong Kong, the present bishop, Gilbert Baker, was in his first period of service in the Diocese of Canton. He recalls that Leonard and Mary came like a breath of fresh air into the then fairly stuffy life of the cathedral and the community. R. O. Hall was already beginning to make himself that greatly respected bishop who came to be so much beloved by Christians in China. The two played a very happy complementary part in the work. Gilbert Baker writes:

They were remarkably different in their approach, though basically in agreement. R.O., though amazingly outgoing, with his quick mind, boldness of planning and deep concern for people, yet had his ascetic side. He didn't like parties or mixing up with Europeans, partly because he felt it was detracting from the Chinese side of his work, but also because he was shy and rather bored by them. Leonard was quite different, loved a party, warmed up to people very quickly, and with him you felt that to be a Christian was a natural and right position for a man of the world.

With his usual energy and drive Leonard threw himself into the life of the cathedral and the diocese. He was always on good terms with the Chinese clergy, though he never mastered their language. He used to address the late Archdeacon Lee Kau Yan as 'Wooly John', which was the nearest he could get to the Cantonese word for archdeacon 'wooi lei-cheung'. His main work was with the British. He soon made his mark in the cathedral. His conviction that the Christian faith was not the preserve of 'religious' people, but that here was a message of love and truth for the hearts and minds of ordinary, intelligent people, and his power to present it as such, found a ready response in his congregation. Here, as elsewhere, there were some who did not approve of the dean's easy social graces, but Leonard liked eating with publicans and sinners for the best of all reasons, that he enjoyed their company. When he went to a party at the sergeants' mess of the Durham Light Infantry wearing his regimental tie, he tried to get the band to play *Blaydon Races*, but they couldn't. So he got up and sang it himself, and got them all singing it.

When Bishop Baker was at Kunming, Leonard and Mary spent a few days with him. He showed them the walled city and the remarkable temples on the lake outside the city, but what Leonard enjoyed most was an informal buffet supper with some of the western community, British and American, and joining in choruses, some slightly ribald, while their host played his guitar. Occasions of this kind were spontaneous expressions of his liking for all sorts of people. He was well aware of the dignity of office, but he never fell into the mistake of being pompous about it. This is a balance which it is not always easy to preserve, and sometimes people found Leonard's attitude difficult to take. When the local community was preparing for the centenary celebrations in Hong Kong, the man in charge was irritated with Leonard, and said, 'We've been here thirty years, and you've only been here eighteen months and lecture us on what we ought to do.' Leonard answered, 'Well, in thirty years I've lived in four big cities, so I really do know a lot more about the world than you do. Come and have some dinner with me.'

On one occasion Leonard received a letter from the Secretary at Government House,

My dear Dean,

Two members of the Executive Council observed this morning that you did not use the words 'Sir' and 'Your Excellency' when addressing the Governor. I fear I never noticed anything myself, and should not mention it even if I did. But I only averted a 'by direction' letter from the Clerk of Councils by promising to let you know about it, which unpleasant duty is now fulfilled. I hope it will be forgotten on both sides.

When the Wilsons first arrived in Hong Kong, there was no official residence for the dean. For two years they lived in rented houses, constantly moving from one part of Hong Kong to another. On two occasions they were lent the Governor's summer residence on top of the Peak for a few months in the winter. Representations were constantly being made to the Government for a site on which to build a deanery, but land was in short supply and nothing happened. At last, Leonard got impatient and asked for an interview with the Governor. He obtained this and the Governor said, 'Now, Mr. Dean, what can

I do for you?' Leonard replied, 'Lord, that I might receive my site.' It was not long after this that the Wilsons got their deanery, and as further evidence that the Governor, Sir Stafford Northcote, was favourably impressed by Leonard, when the question of the Bishopric of Singapore came up, and soundings were being made, he said of Leonard, 'He's the wisest head I've got in the Colony.'

One other story from this time, told by Bishop Hall, is worth recording. Madame Su Yat Sen and her two sisters had a base for their operations in Hong Kong. They put on a film called *Pastor Hall*, which showed a German pastor being tortured by the Nazis for his beliefs. She invited Bishop Hall to go and see it. He took Leonard with him and at the end of the film, Leonard said, 'Thank you, R.O., I feel I have been witnessing the Crucifixion.'

In the autumn of 1939 a number of women and children were evacuated from Hong Kong to Australia, among them Mary Wilson and her two children, Susan and Timothy. Leonard went with the party to look after their needs and help settle them in their new homes. He stayed in Australia until April 1940, when their son Martin was born, and then returned to Hong Kong. As we have seen, it was in March 1941 that he accepted Lang's offer of the Bishopric of Singapore. In the summer of the same year Leonard went to Bowral to pick up the family and take them to Singapore. Leonard and Mary left the children there when they went back to Hong Kong for two weeks for Leonard's consecration.

CHAPTER 7

The Years Between

WHEN LEONARD JOINED MARY and the children at Bowral in New South Wales in October 1945, he had been separated from them for more than three and a half years. He had never seen his youngest son, James, now three years old. Susan was eleven, Timothy nine, and Martin five. Except for one or two brief messages there had been no communication between Leonard and his family.

Family ties were always important to Leonard, and perhaps one of the results of his long separation from his children was that they became more self-consciously so. The months which followed were a time of physical and mental relaxation. The family spent Christmas at Bowral, and Leonard made short visits to Melbourne and Sydney. Naturally he was much in request as a speaker, and he did several talks for the Australian Broadcasting Commission, including one for Easter Day. In this he linked his own past experiences with the faith that the universe is governed by a God who is continually bringing new life out of suffering and death, and giving new hope not only for individual men and women, but also for the peoples of the world 'as they emerge from the chaos, degradation and bitterness of the pains of war'.

In February Leonard and Mary paid a visit to New Zealand at the invitation of the Board of Missions and he preached at the General Synod and on the radio. In October he had received a letter from the Archbishop of Canterbury, in which Fisher wrote:

> From many quarters I have received most moving testimonies to your fortitude under extreme torture and to the wonderful impression which your Christian witness and courage had made not only in Singapore but throughout Malaya. Today Hayter came to see me and I have had the whole story again at first hand. No words of mine can be adequate, but I do want you to know that we at home immensely appreciate at its full worth all that you have suffered and done. It is wonderful to hear from Hayter that you have recovered your health and good spirits, but there must come a reaction and I am thankful that you are taking two or three months' rest with your family in Australia. In due course we shall be able to welcome you here in England. When the time comes for you to return to Singapore what a heritage of good-will there you have earned for yourself and for the Christian Faith.

In the course of his reply Leonard wrote, 'I was a little overworked when I first came out of internment, doing relieving work in Malaya, consequently I am overtired now, and do not seem to think as straightly as I would like . . . I am greatly enjoying the loveliness of being reunited with my family, and the good fellowship and friendliness of the Australian Church.'

Leonard and his family left for England in March 1946. During the following six months, he fulfilled a great many speaking engagements in different parts of the country. In May he was received in audience by the King, and in July he was invested with the C.M.G. On Sunday, October 13th, he broadcast in the Home Service of the B.B.C. A number of extracts from this sermon have already been quoted. In it he set out simply and movingly the story of his internment and torture and what these had done for his Christian faith. He said, 'It is not my purpose to relate the tortures they inflicted upon us, but rather to tell you of some of the spiritual experiences of that ordeal. I knew this was to be a challenge to my courage, my faith and my love.' And he ended with this confession of faith:

God is to be found in the Resurrection, as well as in the Cross, and it is the Resurrection that has the final word. God in all his power and strength and comfort is available to every one of us today. He was revealed to me not because I was a special person, but because I was willing in faith to accept what God gave. I know it is true not just because the Bible says so, or because the Church has told us, but because I have experienced it myself; and whether you are despondent or in joy, whether you are apathetic or full of enthusiasm, there is available for you at this moment the whole life of God with its victory over sin and pain and death.

These words are really the key to understanding the influence that Leonard had, and to the love and regard in which he was held by all sorts and conditions of men and women. He was convinced that the grace of our Lord Jesus Christ, the love of God and the fellowship of the Holy Spirit were the ultimate truths of the human situation, and he was able, in many different ways, to share this certainty with others so that they too recognised that the Resurrection has the final word'.

In November Leonard went to see Hensley Henson, the Bishop of Durham, for whom he had a great respect and affection all his life. Henson recorded the visit in his diary.

Leonard Wilson, the Bishop of Singapore ('whose praise is in the churches' for his admirable behaviour when abominably tortured by the Japanese, into whose hands he fell when they captured Singapore) with his wife, called in the afternoon. I had some conversation with him, and was well impressed by the good sense and self-restraint of his answers to my questions. He told me that the Anglican Christians had come through the 'great tribulation' with special credit, that the Episcopal Methodists, who were the most numerous among the non-episcopal converts, were weakened by their internecine disputes, in which he had himself been often invited to intervene as peacemaker. He thought it very desirable that the South India Scheme of Reunion should be carried into effect . . . Leonard Wilson's career is remarkable, and, as an indication of tendencies within the English Church, significant. He began his ministry as a C.M.S. missionary in Egypt, where he became disgusted with the crude literalism which marked the Society's understanding of the Bible. He parted company with it, and came back to England under the cloud of its bigoted disapproval. Canon Holland (now Dean of Norwich) sent him to me as a man known to be friendly to mental freedom, and I welcomed him in the Durham Diocese. Now he is Bishop of Singapore and revered as a Confessor of the Faith. (Hensley Henson: *Retrospect of an Unimportant Life*.)

The broadcast of October brought Leonard hundreds of letters, and it was later incorporated into a booklet, produced and distributed by a few of his friends, to help the appeal for the Diocese of Singapore. Leonard set out to raise a hundred thousand pounds. In his appeal he emphasised the need for schools which could be centres for the tradition of Christian community service. This would mean training the right kind of teachers, and placing the schools in strategic positions. There was a need for specialised medical work, which would supplement the government health services by pioneer work in spheres where these did not yet operate. There was also the need to provide centres of community life, and this meant the building of halls with facilities for recreation, study and discussion. The immediate aims were to re-equip the Home for Blind Children and Hospital for Crippled Children; to rebuild and replace war-damaged churches and halls; to rebuild and furnish the mission schools; to provide a chapel and school for lepers; to provide a general hospital for women's work; and to build a hall for the cathedral.

These were some of the tasks which faced Leonard when he returned to Singapore in November 1946, and occupied him for the next fifteen months. It was not an easy time. Writing to a friend some eighteen months later he said:

I had one of the most miserable six months that I have ever experienced when I went back to Malaya. All the enthusiasm seemed to have gone dead, and there were one or two very old friends who seemed to have changed so much as to be different people. The effort of trying to reconstruct when money was so short and everyone was so tired was a great strain.

The work towards Christian unity which he had done much to further in the year before he was interned moved more slowly than he would have liked. In the same letter, he wrote, 'People are beginning to settle down again into their ruts of denominationalism, and it isn't easy to rouse them to the creation of a wider vision and a more united front.' However, there were some more hopeful signs. He had been well supported in his efforts to establish a united training college for church workers and clergy, and in the formation of a Malayan Christian Council, so that he was able to add in the same letter, 'The last three or four months of my stay there showed a very great improvement, and I came away knowing that from a human point of view things were developing splendidly.' When, at the end of 1948, it became known in Singapore that Leonard was to go to Manchester, the heads of both the Methodists and the English Presbyterian Missions wrote to him to say how important they thought was the work of the united college, which had doubled its membership, and which owed its existence to Leonard's vision, sympathetic attitude and whole-hearted co-operation.

By the end of March 1948 Leonard was back in England. He was kept very busy, and lamented the fact that there were so few opportunities for the family to be together. Leslie Hunter, the Bishop of Sheffield, invited him to join his pre-Lambeth Conference group. He put Leonard to stay with one of the best doctors in Sheffield, who was astonished that he was as fit as he was. Writing to a friend in Singapore, Leonard said:

I was very glad that I got home in time to see Susan and Timothy, but we have not been together as a family for more than three hours. I have had little time to read the newspaper. I have done no light reading at all. It is a very hectic existence but I continue to get funds in for the diocese, and I am keeping very fit, although I had a bad patch in the middle of the Lambeth campaign. I meet Mary and go to Canterbury today for the inaugural service at the cathedral for the Lambeth Conference. I had a very pleasant day off last week with Padre Steel when we discussed diocesan business at Lord's. From England's point of view the Test Match was disastrous, but it was interesting cricket.

Shortly after the Lambeth Conference, Leonard received a letter from his old friend Bishop Hall in which he said:

I have come to realise it was your insistence that I should go to the U.S.A. in 1941 for those lectures that saved me from your terrible experiences, and gave me the chance to be some use to the Chinese Church as a whole. I thought I might remind you of that, and beg you to remember that sometimes to appear to be ungallant may be what God wants. I am more and more convinced that England needs you: for the rest of the younger men seemed to be able exponents of the obvious: the mixture as before in more attractive bottles.

This is not to be answered: and please not to worry you. I trust your judgment more than mine. But it was I who dragged you out of England, and I long to help to get you back.

More than a year before this, Hall had said in the course of a letter to Leonard, 'You will have heard that Billy (Greer) goes to Manchester. I have set him another task: to get you to England, either to succeed him at Westcott, or Barnes at Birmingham.'

It is clear that by the time the bishops assembled at Lambeth in 1948, Leslie Hunter was trying to secure him as Provost of Sheffield. Leonard refused the offer on the ground that he did not feel certain that the time had come for him to leave Singapore. Hunter wrote to Fisher asking the latter to tell Leonard that he ought to accept. Fisher wrote to Leonard saying it was difficult for him to issue a direction of that kind. The difficulty was increased by the fact that Fisher had reason to suppose that another offer of work of a comparable kind in England would shortly come to him, which would in Fisher's view have a stronger claim than the provostship of Sheffield. While leaving Leonard quite free to balance the advantages between making use of the immense goodwill he had created in Malaya on the one hand, and taking up important work in England while he was still young and fresh enough for it, he suggested it might be best to hold his hand as the other offer he had referred to might come along soon, and, if it did, Leonard probably ought to accept it.

It is clear that the usual game of hide-and-seek which is played in the corridors of power about high-up appointments in the Church of England was in full swing. Greer was very anxious that Leonard should join him at Manchester as dean in succession to Garfield Williams who was going to resign in November. This was, of course, the other offer to which Fisher had referred. Leonard must have known about it when he got Fisher's letter, and it is highly probable that Fisher knew that Leonard knew when he wrote. Six days after Fisher had written, Leonard had a letter from Attlee saying he proposed to submit Leonard's name to the King for the Deanery of Manchester if he would be willing to accept. Leonard felt himself to be in a difficult position. Hunter was on holiday in Switzerland and was still hoping that Leonard would go to Sheffield.

Leonard talked to Greer on the telephone, and the latter with characteristic openness and generosity decided to write direct to Hunter. Reporting this to Leonard he said:

I have explained how the present situation has arisen and told him that I suggested you might defer your final decision till he returns.

I think, if I were you, I would write to the Prime Minister, and say you hoped he would not mind your delaying your decision till say September 30th, as you had been approached by the Bishop of Sheffield about another appointment and he was out of the country till the 27th. I don't think you should go to Sheffield to prevent L.S.H. from feeling 'let down', only if you see clearly that it is God's will for you. I think you need this caution because (although you are of course a notorious modernist) your heart can easily run away with your head! The same I may say applies to Manchester (I mean the job not the bishop). God guide you. I shall pray that you may be able to make the decision in light and not in darkness. Or perhaps it is the light comes once the decision is made.

However disappointed he may have been on personal grounds Hunter willingly released Leonard from any feeling of guilt about Sheffield, and at the end of September Leonard wrote to the Prime Minister that he was willing to accept the Deanery of Manchester if the King approved. At the same time he wrote to Fisher:

I am most grateful for the careful consideration that you gave to the problem of my future work and have accepted your advice, having told the Prime Minister that I am willing to go as Dean of Manchester.

I am returning to Singapore on October 12th, as I feel there ought to be a month or two's work in clearing up such matters so as to leave a clear field for my successor, and I think I am technically in order in asking you to accept my resignation from the Bishopric of Singapore as from March 31st, 1949. This will involve three or four months' vacancy at Manchester, but I have explained the position to the bishop and as I have many Confirmations waiting in Singapore, and a meeting of the newly formed Synod in January, I doubt if it will be possible to fulfil what I consider the minimum duties before the end of February.

Reconstruction was at first extremely difficult, but in spite of the new troubles in Malaya the work seems to be going apace. If only I could get the men and the money to seize the opportunities which are now open to us. It will be sad to say goodbye to friendships which have been made steadfast in the school of affliction, but since I received your letter I have become increasingly aware of my personal desires to be with my family of four children, and although this would not have influenced my judgment without your advice on other grounds, I am beginning to enjoy the prospect of seeing something of them.

Leonard left by boat for Singapore on October 12th. It had been agreed that the appointment would be published on October 18th, but the authorities agreed to Leonard's sending a confidential message through the Colonial Office to the Assistant Chaplain-General, who was administering the diocese, giving the news and asking him to inform diocesan officials confidentially and the evening congregation at the cathedral on October 17th. The message stated, 'After much consideration and following the advice of my Metropolitan I have accepted Deanery of Manchester. Will greatly regret leaving Singapore. Am returning for Confirmations and Synod.'

There was plenty to be done in the few months left to him. The Diocesan Council met for the last time in December, and the new Synod for the first time in January. Leonard was taking Confirmations, assessing the needs of the diocese, and sending full information to the archbishop with regard to the appointment of his successor. He had never felt entirely at ease in Singapore from his first return in November 1946. Of the seven years in which he was bishop, he had only had about eighteen months of more or less normal conditions. As we have seen, he felt disappointed and frustrated that his hopes for greater Christian unity after the testing years of war and internment were not quickly fulfilled.

Leonard himself may have found it unusually difficult to settle down to the kind of humdrum diocesan administration which the years after the war demanded. However that may be, there is no doubt that his old friend Sorby Adams, spoke for many when he wrote to Leonard:

It was with a little sadness that I caught a note in your voice last Monday suggesting that not all in this diocese had welcomed or appreciated your services here. I would like you to know that I myself feel that you have contributed a very great deal to our life and more especially to our outlook. I feel certain that when you have given so much of what you have stood for (and so earnestly prayed for) in the way of a wider conception of life, and of the family spirit in the whole Church of God, this spirit will, in time, be appreciated by us, your children in God.

I have seen the expression of human-divine-love in your dealings with many. The latest of these was with that dear man Daniels from Kelantan. He is a very dear person and he for one will, whether he realises it or not, carry into his work that same spirit. In this same spirit I give you my love and such blessings as you need and I may give.

At Christmas, Leonard wrote again to Fisher with further information about the needs of the diocese and included the following about his own plans, 'I shall be home about February 20th. I have ordered myself a Retreat with the Franciscans at Cerne Abbas from March 1st to 4th, in preparation for the

111

protestantism of my new post at Manchester, where I am to be installed on March 23rd.'

On January 30th he broadcast a farewell message in Singapore:

I am very grateful for this opportunity of saying farewell from this studio. The studio has pleasant memories and historic associations. It was from this building that I conducted one of the last services before the Japanese occupation. It was from here that those who had been interned gave their first message to the outside world, when on their behalf I thanked God for our liberation. It was from this studio that I preached the best sermon I have ever preached, but, alas, it was not my own. The words were those which T. S. Eliot puts into the mouth of Thomas à Beckett in the play *Murder in the Cathedral*. And now I am here for the last time, and I find it difficult to select the appropriate words to clothe the conflicting thoughts that occupy my mind.

I am saying farewell to friends, firm friends, made during eleven years in the Far East both here and in Hong Kong; to many happy and memorable associations; and to the work I have loved and tried to set forward during the interrupted years of my episcopate. Few people know better than I do how inadequate that work has been, and although I have tried to fulfil my task without fear or favour, I seem hardly to have begun it before I am bidden to lay it down, and seek fresh woods and pastures new: though that, I am led to understand, is a grossly exaggerated description of Manchester. My leaving does not mean that the ties that bind me to this country will be severed. No separation could do that, for not only has more than half my active ministry been spent in the East, but much the most eventful part of it. For it would not be possible for me to omit all reference to those years that so often at the time seemed a long descent of wasted days, but which, I now realise, helped me to learn and understand much that would, in outwardly more happy times, have been hidden from me. The years that the locusts have eaten have been restored, and my imprisonment is not to be recorded in the chronicles of wasted time. Adversity and war are a great test of our moral and spiritual resources, and I learned much of, and was helped much by, those who endured so well the helpless tedium of internment.

My years in Malaya have taught me one thing above all else; the necessity of living without rancour and bitterness. I don't always remember that lesson, but whenever I forget it, chaos comes back again. Stevenson gives us a rule of life that, the older I get and the more I experience, I know more firmly to be true. 'We must grant absolution to ourselves and to all men each night, and begin each new day with a clean sheet.' Now, more than ever, in a world divided and insecure, we cannot afford the luxury of quarrelling.

'Purge from every heart the lurking grudge.' I have rejected all the other things I was going to say to the various and friendly communities of Malaya, both racial and religious, and I prefer to give to all the message of that simple line, 'Purge from every heart the lurking grudge.'

Last Sunday I saw again what is for me the fairest sight in all the Far East, the lovely view from Penang Hill, of islands, sea and distant peak; last night I watched the light of the setting sun on the waters of MacRitchie reservoir and saw most vividly 'the long low splendour of the level lake'. Here are things of beauty which one need not obliterate, because they are to be enjoyed for ever, being part of the Divine Nature of the Eternal God. I shall take away from Malaya not only memories of this beautiful country, not only truths I have learned from all communities, but also, thank God, the love of many loyal friends.

May the Peace of God be with you tonight and always.

Two days later, Leonard sailed for home.

CHAPTER 8

Manchester

IT IS SAD, if salutary, to reflect how often the cathedral close has been the scene of clerical rivalry and bitterness. It has provided more than one writer of detective fiction with a rich setting for his murder story, not to mention all those novelists who have borrowed from the Trollope tradition. Perhaps the combination of beautiful buildings, rich music, and a position of authority makes it particularly difficult for those who enjoy these privileges to accept the Pauline warning to do nothing through faction, but with the humility in which each counts the other better than himself. Certainly there was more than enough faction in the cathedral Chapter at Manchester in the years that Leonard was dean, and it is equally certain that the faults were not all on one side.

Leonard had high hopes of what he might do in Manchester. Here was a place in which the cathedral could play a leading part in that revival of Christian faith and action which had been the key-note of the Lambeth Conference. All through his life, at Coventry, in the North of England, in Cairo, in Hong Kong and Singapore, he had been able to get alongside those outside the organised life of the Church. He knew and loved north country people. He had been through experiences which very few clergy had ever shared. As has already been said, what mattered most about these was the way in which they had confirmed him in his own Christian faith and conviction. But he cannot have been unaware that they had made him something of a national hero, and he would have been less than human had he not felt that this was an added advantage in the work he hoped to do in Manchester. The last two years in Singapore had been something of an anticlimax. Now he had the chance of a new setting for his hopes and gifts with the background of a home and family life to be enjoyed together for the first time.

The canons of the cathedral were ready to give Leonard a welcome, but they were men of a very different stamp and they had held their positions for a long time. They had held the fort through the difficult years of the war and the post-war period. The cathedral had been badly damaged in the air-raids of 1941, and they were faced with numerous practical difficulties. More importantly, the kind of approach to the spiritual and pastoral needs of the city, which the new post-war situation demanded, was different from what had been successful in earlier days in a different climate of thought. If it was only human in Leonard to see his new post as a great chance for outgoing experiments and adventures, it was equally only human that they should wish to guard and protect a tradition which they had built up and in which they believed. If Leonard had been more tactful, and they had been less conscious of their proper rights, things might have worked out better. But the committee situation was never one in which Leonard evinced more than a minimal capacity for tact, and the canons were not able to make an exception in his case to their feeling that, while deans may make good diocesan bishops, diocesan bishops make bad deans.

Under the cathedral statutes the dean was *primus inter pares*. While the dean had considerable powers of veto, any positive plans had to have the agreement of the Chapter. Except for the greater festivals, the Canon in Residence was in charge of the statutory services, and if Leonard wanted to officiate or to invite a preacher for these, he could only do so with the consent of the Canon in Residence. Leonard was always an individualist not a team man, and what was a strength in one set of circumstances was a weakness in another. In personal relationships he was at

115

his best, and his best was of a very high quality, but in official relationships he was often difficult and touchy. The humility and grace, which characterised his human relationships, sometimes deserted him when he chaired official meetings, and his opinions were opposed or his judgment questioned. It seemed as if he was sure of himself as a person, but had unconscious doubts about himself as a man under authority. It was this which made him unpredictable, particularly when the relationship was both personal and official. On such occasions his manner might be either distant or intimate, and it would be difficult for the other person to know on which wicket he was batting. One who had known him both as an undergraduate and as a bishop remarked that Leonard had a very independent mind; the things he said were seventy-five per cent predictable and twenty-five per cent completely unpredictable. He was able at times to be strongly self-assertive; he was equally able to be very gentle and generous. His time as Dean of Manchester revealed both these sides of his character.

For the first six months after their arrival in Manchester Leonard and his family occupied a flat, but in September they were able to move into the house which was bought as a deanery, in St. Anne's Road, Prestwich. This new home became the background for that hospitality for which Leonard and Mary had such an outstanding gift. Many who were in trouble or loneliness found here a warmth of family affection which was in itself a comfort and inspiration. There were also happy parties for both grown-ups and children. On such occasions Leonard was at ease and happy, and his spirit was infectious. Greer and Leonard ran a Christmas party at a Manchester hotel for the small children of the clergy of the diocese, and Leonard was the life and soul of the occasion. One year there was a convention of the clergy at Swanwick. The lighter side of this gathering included a topical skit based on Hamlet. Leonard played the part of Ophelia in an extremely skittish costume.

The cathedral needed £90,000 for restoration work over and

above what was paid by the War Damage Commission. The appeal had been started before Leonard arrived, but he was responsible for raising a large proportion of it, and for guiding the plans and those concerned with them at different stages of the work. By June 1952, £83,900 had been raised, and on a Friday at the end of that month, Leonard sat at the west door of the cathedral from 7.30 a.m. to 6.30 p.m. to receive gifts. This effort brought in £2,400, and the target was reached some few weeks later.

In spite of the unhappy and sometimes stormy relationships in the Chapter, Leonard was able to make a valuable contribution to the inner life of the cathedral. The Sunday evening nave service was in his hands, and he strengthened and widened its popularity. Those who remember him officiating at the cathedral services recall, as many others have done in other places, how impressively he combined dignity, a great sense of meaning, and beautiful clarity of diction. He also had a deep concern for those who worked in the cathedral. On one occasion the visiting preacher had asked the verger to turn off the pulpit microphone. The verger forgot and the preacher's voice came out in a boom. In the vestry after the service, the man said to the verger, 'I asked you to turn the microphone off, and you forgot.' Leonard overheard the remark and said at once, 'I'm the dean. If you have any complaints, tell me. I will pass them on to those concerned.'

If Leonard's activity as dean was limited, he found a great deal to do outside, in the city, in the diocese, helping with Confirmations and in other ways, and with many engagements outside which took him all over the country. He was a welcome guest at civic dinners; he was a Freemason; he became a member of the Clerical Advisory Board of the National Marriage Guidance Council; he was chairman of the Manchester branch of the Council of Christians and Jews; and he succeeded Sir Ernest Bullock as chairman of the Royal School of Church Music. What was important to Leonard about these various activities was that they were the means of widening his contacts with individuals in different walks of life. Canon Sheild, who was Diocesan Missioner, recalls:

We both wished to get closer to ordinary men, to make friends with them, and to understand more about their approach to religion. Sometimes we met for lunch at a small public house in a back street where a snack lunch was served at the bar and where we enjoyed (sometimes incognito, sometimes not) mingling with the other customers and chatting with them. I think the public house was called *The Fatted Calf*! What attracted me most in him was his dislike of humbug. He had the gift of easy informality, yet he graced formal occasions, for example a Royal visit to the cathedral, with impressive dignity.

Early in 1950 Leonard was approached by Bishop Roberts, then Secretary of the S.P.G., to see if he would take part in the two hundred and fiftieth anniversary celebrations of the Society in the following year. Special envoys were to be sent out on tours of goodwill to overseas churches, and Leonard was invited to go to South and West Africa. On the receipt of this invitation, Leonard wrote as follows:

My dear Bishop Roberts,

I have received your letter this morning and I thank you for inviting me to represent the S.P.G. next year.

I notice with a certain amount of shrinking that you have offered me the field of South and West Africa. I am, of course, ready to go wherever the Society thinks it right for me to go, but I feel I ought to point out that I might not be altogether *persona grata* in the province of South Africa because of my opposition to the Apartheid policies, and I should find it difficult to compromise on this. I would, as far as I can control these things, go without prejudice to the many difficult situations that arise in any country where conflicting opinions are so conscientiously held . . . I feel that the colour bar question

118

is one of the things on which I cannot compromise, and though I would not take this opportunity of entering into controversies, situations may arise in which I might be compelled on conscientious grounds to take some action which might be embarrassing either to my hosts or to the Society I represented.

South Africa is the place above all others which seems to need tactful and delicate handling even by a cursory visitor. My tread might be a little elephantine. If, however, you and your committee still feel that I am the right person for the job, I will gladly and willingly undertake the task and try to copy Agag.

In his reply Bishop Roberts set out the guiding principles which the Society would wish to follow. The object was to send messages of greeting and goodwill and not to implicate itself in the controversial affairs of the Province; the official voice of the Province was assumed to be opposed to race segregation, and with that opposition S.P.G. would feel sympathy and concurrence; the Archbishop of Canterbury had said publicly that the primary responsibility for this moral issue must lie with the Province of South Africa and the Church of England ought not to intervene, unless invited to do so; it would hardly be consistent with these intentions for a visitor to launch an open attack upon the Government or upon the attitude of other Christian bodies.

Leonard replied that he would certainly conform to these principles, 'Although I have my doubts about the complete wisdom of the archbishop's public announcement.' And so, in April 1951, he left England for West Africa and was away until the end of June. It was a very busy two and a half months. He flew with Fisher to Sierra Leone for the inauguration of the new Province of West Africa, and, at the beginning of May left for Johannesburg. There followed an eight weeks' tour in which he visited all the main towns in the Province of South Africa, preaching every Sunday, addressing meetings, visiting schools and missionary centres.

When in 1953 the question of a Central African Federation was in the forefront of colonial policy, Leonard chaired a meeting in Manchester addressed by two Nyasaland Chiefs, Dr. Hastings Banda, and the Reverend Michael Scott. Leonard said he thought that some of the suggested federation policies had aroused so much fear and apprehension that they should not be put into operation until this fear had been dispelled and mutual confidence established. He went on to say:

> These Chiefs and representatives have come to plead their cause before the British public. The funds for their journey have been provided, not by the rich people with axes to grind, but from thousands, perhaps millions, of poor people who feel, not so much that their livelihood is in danger, but that their whole way of life is threatened. They ask for nothing more than to remain at the present time in our care, that our Government through the Colonial Office should continue their trust and responsibility, and if the British people will say clearly that they are willing to honour their trust, then these representatives will go back to their countries ready to allay their fears, and to help re-establish the confidence we are in danger of losing if we have not already done so.

At a meeting of the S.P.C.K. a few weeks later, the Archbishop of Canterbury said that he had seen it suggested that Christian people should be called upon to pray against federation, and he thought it was a terrible suggestion. Christians differed on the merits of federation and on the more difficult matter of the merits of applying or not applying federation in the immediate future. Someone told Fisher that Leonard had given his name in support of a call to prayer against federation. As Fisher's informant was 'a person who occupies a very responsible position', he felt he had to write to Leonard and check on this.

Leonard replied, 'You ask for a simple and short answer as to whether I had given my name in support of a call to prayer against federation. The answer is "No", and to the best of my knowledge I have not even been asked to do so.' He enclosed a copy of the notes for his speech for the meeting held in Manchester and went on, 'On reading these through I stand amazed at my own moderation. I hope there is enough in my letter to give you further evidence that people "in very responsible positions" do sometimes make very irresponsible statements which cause you to be bothered.'

Fisher's slightly enigmatic reply was, 'Thank you very much for your reply which told me the kind of thing I expected to hear from you. It enables me to assure the person in high position that he was totally misinformed.'

A little later in the same year Leonard received an invitation from Lord Hemingford to become an Honorary President of the Africa Bureau, which Leonard gladly accepted.

In 1953 Bishop Barnes resigned from Birmingham. On June 2nd, Leonard received a letter from the Prime Minister offering him the post. Leonard immediately consulted with Greer. They were old friends and Leonard wanted his personal counsel as well as his official opinion as his bishop. Greer had no desire to lose Leonard, but he knew some of the frustrations that surrounded his life as dean, and he felt strongly that Leonard was the right person to go to Birmingham. Leonard asked Greer if the archbishop knew that the offer was to be made and whether he approved, and Greer told Leonard that Fisher did know and did approve. Accordingly Leonard replied to the Prime Minister on June 5th saying that he was willing for his name to be submitted to the Queen. Fisher was annoyed that Leonard had allowed his name to go forward before consulting him and wrote to Leonard on June 9th. This letter does not survive, but Leonard's reply, written the following day, was as follows:

Thank you very much for your letter, dated June 9th, and for your kindness in writing to me.

The Prime Minister's letter was written some ten days ago and I assumed was sent with your approval and goodwill. I had a long talk with my bishop about it and wrote to the Prime Minister saying that, if Her Majesty approved of his nomination, I felt it my duty to accept.

I told my bishop that I had some reluctance both on the grounds of my fitness to take on such heavy responsibilities and, less worthily, to tackle what I considered a difficult job.

I would greatly welcome your help and guidance and put myself at your disposal to see you at your convenience.

Twelve days later, on June 22nd, after the appointment had been made public, Fisher wrote two letters to Leonard. In the first he said that he had wanted to reply to Leonard's letter as soon as it came but extreme pressure of work had made it impossible. He would be sending an invitation for him to attend the Bishops' Meetings on July 7th and 8th, and he hoped to arrange a talk with Leonard on one of those days. The second letter contained the invitation to the Bishops' Meetings, assuring him that he would be warmly welcomed, and advising him of the advantages of putting up at the hostel in the Palace, 'the cheapest hotel available in London'. On the receipt of these letters Leonard replied at once:

Very few things have distressed me so much over my appointment to the See of Birmingham than to hear from my bishop of your displeasure that I had not consulted you before accepting.

When I first received the letter from the Prime Minister, I consulted my bishop and one of the first things I asked him was whether you knew of the offer and whether you thought it my duty to accept. In both cases the answer was clearly, 'Yes'. As he himself was of the same opinion I felt there was little more to be said.

I have always taken the line that all clergy should be much more mobile and be under orders which were informed and reasonable, so I did not consult my own desires or those of my family: if I had, my answer would have been very different. Hearing from the Bishop of Manchester that you wanted me to go, I accepted.

I thought it would have been discourteous to bother you at a time when your duties were distracting and almost overwhelming. Of course I would have liked to have seen you; of course I would have liked to have had your blessing or any rate been assured of it; and indeed, most unwittingly, I have caused you to be troubled. I can only say that I am sorry it should have happened thus and I will gladly avail myself of the chance of seeing you at Lambeth on July 7th or 8th. I have written to the warden asking if it is possible for me to have accommodation.

In the meanwhile, I shall not commit myself to any line of action or consultation until I have received your advice and guidance.

Fisher answered by return in his own handwriting:

It was very good and kind of you to write so generously. We can now most cheerfully forget the matter altogether. As usual in such things, everyone meant the right thing. Any trouble arose simply on what might and what might not be 'assumed'. Anyhow all is now clear. I am very glad that you can come to the Bishops' Meetings and we can have a talk during them. Forgive the irregularities of a pen I am not used to!

Those who have worked in a school know it is unwise for assistant masters to assume that they know what is in the headmaster's mind.

In September Leonard preached his farewell sermon in Manchester Cathedral, and began to make ready for his move to Harborne and to the house which was to be his family home for the next sixteen years.

CHAPTER 9

Birmingham

I   SUCCESSOR TO BISHOP BARNES

By an Order in Council of January 12th, 1905, the new diocese of Birmingham was created, and a week later it was announced that Charles Gore, who had done so much to make this possible, was to be its first bishop. Gore was followed in 1911 by Wakefield, whose episcopate covered the years of the First World War and the immediate post-war period. He resigned early in 1924, and on Michaelmas Day in the same year, Ernest William Barnes was consecrated in Westminster Abbey as the third Bishop of Birmingham.

It is a great pity that up to the present time no biography of Barnes has been written. He was an outstanding figure in the religious life of this country, and the record of the Church of England in the second quarter of this century is incomplete without a true assessment of his contribution to its history, both as Bishop of Birmingham and as a catalyst in a period of rapidly changing religious views.

In the heated controversy which often surrounded the words and actions of Barnes, it was apt to be forgotten what a gentle and imaginative pastor he was. He was the embodiment of courtesy and courage, and there is no doubt that the background to both was his deep and simple faith in Christ as Lord and Saviour.

In October 1928, the writer went, at Barnes's invitation, to take charge of the new district of St. Mark's, Londonderry,

Smethwick. *The Smethwick Telephone* gave a full report of Barnes's address when the new building was dedicated. This shows that Barnes and Leonard, whose backgrounds were so dissimilar, shared one important quality. They were both committed to a simple evangelical faith, which was deeply rooted in their hearts and upheld them in the time of trial and persecution, though the outward forms of these were so very different.

In his address Barnes said:

We have the site; we have this building. And that is at the moment all, save for the faith that is in us, the confident trust that God will bless those who honestly seek to show His power and His love to the men and women of our land and who desire to spread the spirit of His Son, their Saviour Jesus Christ. I would have you remember that this building exists primarily that you may spread here, and hereabouts, a knowledge of the teaching and love of our Saviour. We desire men, women and children to be drawn to Him, as we learn of His greatness, of the beauty of His message, of the range of His knowledge, of His power unto salvation. We believe that without the stimulus, the enthusiasm, the confidence, which the Christian faith alone can give to life, it becomes dreary, blank, sometimes sordid or vicious.

In welcoming the Mayor of Smethwick and representatives of civic authorities, Barnes went on:

I desire, continually, to emphasise that there is no antagonism between the Church and the State, between those who seek equally to do God's service by spreading ideals of social happiness, of civic virtue through the agencies which they in turn can command. Civic authorities and religious enthusiasts ought to be able, together, to build up in our land something which has behind it the vision of the Kingdom of God.

He then went on to say that he had noticed in that day's

papers it was proposed to extend the teaching of science in Birmingham's elementary schools. After expressing the hope that the same development would take place in the Borough of Smethwick, he said:

It may be that much of the science thus learned will be forgotten in after years, just as many of the details of religion learned in Sunday Schools are forgotten. But none the less there is good hope that the scientific attitude of mind will be permanent, just as we trust, through Sunday School teaching, followed by steady worship, the religious attitude of mind is sustained . . . Our modern material civilisation is built on the triumphs of science. It is imperfect because we have not managed to permeate it by the ideals of the Kingdom of God . . . I would emphasise that ethical and spiritual religion, Christianity at its highest, has nothing to fear from scientific progress . . . If all the children of our schools could be taught science and at the same time could be given the simple principles and precepts of Christianity, the children would harmonise the two elements of their teaching with unconscious ease, and we would create in England, which we all love, an outlook which would be a sure bond of national cohesion . . . I dream of that era when we will unite all modern culture, which has spread with such immense rapidity during the last hundred years, unite all our visions, our hopes, our ideals, to all those aspirations which we draw from God, through our Lord and Saviour.

It is nearly fifty years since Barnes spoke in these terms. It will seem to many today that there was a certain naïvety about his hopes, and that the intervening years have shown little progress towards the ideal he espoused. That may be true, but it is doubtful if anyone on the Bench of Bishops today, or, for that matter, anyone on any other bench, sees the problem of reconciling traditional Christianity and modern knowledge more clearly than Barnes did, or brings to the task a more deeply rooted and confident hope.

Leonard Wilson was inspired by a similar vision and upheld by a similar hope. He, too, had learnt that the removal of those things that are shaken could not destroy his ultimate trust in the things that cannot be shaken. Both were liberal in mind and spirit. Both, beneath their liberalism, had a simple, deeply rooted faith of the heart, which, though greatly tested, never deserted them. Both were firmly convinced of the reality of personal life after death. At the dedication of the memorial plaque to Barnes in the Cathedral Church of Birmingham, Michael Parker, then Archdeacon of Aston, ended his address with some words from Barnes's Gifford Lectures:

> To no companion on earth's short journey need we give an everlasting farewell. What we begin here we shall finish hereafter, if indeed it be worth finishing. The fact that life is short and precarious matters little, inasmuch as those who have travelled with us here shall be our companions beyond the grave, if we and they alike seek the City of God.

These words could well have been Leonard's.

In his last years Barnes was in declining health, and it is doubtful if he had the strength of body or spirit to deal with many of the practical church difficulties of the post-war situation in Birmingham. New areas were growing fast, and the diocese lacked the manpower and the buildings to meet their needs. Funds were short, and Barnes was hesitant about appeals which he feared might fail. Birmingham accepted Barnes as a great personality, but those concerned with the practical and administrative task of the Church in the city now felt the need for someone to lead them whose major concern would be the future of the diocese rather than the future of Christianity. They were fortunate in the choice of Leonard as successor to Barnes. At his enthronement, Leonard spoke with admiration of both Gore and Barnes. He disclaimed possession of their gifts, but suggested that, better than wishing for gifts that were not his, was his resolve to make the best use of such gifts as he had. It was not long before the people of Birmingham, both those inside the life of the Church and those outside it, realised that in Leonard they had a bishop whose greatest gift was his spontaneous and rich humanity. It was this which won their hearts when he first came to Birmingham, and it was this which they treasured most in their memories of him during the sixteen years he spent among them.

II THE DAILY ROUND

It is not the intention of the present narrative to follow Leonard's years as Bishop of Birmingham in a chronological account of his activities inside and outside the diocese, but rather to try to show the spirit in which he approached his various tasks and how he evaluated them. Much of the detailed work followed the pattern imposed on any diocesan bishop. A large proportion of his time was taken up by official engagements in the diocese. There was the regular round of Confirmations and Institutions of newly appointed incumbents. There were numerous preaching engagements, and Leonard was much in demand as a preacher outside the diocese in all parts of the country. There was a heavy daily correspondence with which to deal, and numerous public meetings, lunches and dinners, where the bishop's interest or patronage was an important part of his public relations. Outside the diocese there were regular attendances at Bishops' Meetings, Convocation and the Church Assembly. These would sometimes involve further meetings as a member of some special committee or commission. When he became a member of the House of Lords he took his turn of weekly duty conducting the opening prayers. From time to time he attended their debates when the subject was one in which he was particularly interested and on which he spoke in the debate. Leonard gave much care and thought to his personal interviews with his own clergy and with many others who sought his advice or help.

Because of his years abroad, Leonard always took a keen interest in what was happening overseas. During his years in Birmingham he made at least fourteen overseas official visits. He went to Canada twice, and twice to the United States. He also visited the West Indies, West Africa, and the Holy Land, and, nearer home, West Germany, France, Holland and Sweden. When Jamaica became independent, the Archbishop of Canterbury was asked to send a representative to attend the celebrations. When the man who was first approached declined, Dr. Ramsey said to Mr. Robert Beloe, 'Ask the Bishop of Birmingham. He enjoys trips.' They did, and Leonard went off with alacrity.

On many of these travels Mary went with Leonard, and the gift they both had of getting alongside all sorts of people and making friends with them, was one of the reasons they were such excellent emissaries for the Church. An example of this was their journey to Minneapolis for the Anglican Conference there in 1954. On their way they stayed with their old friend Gilbert Baker, who was then Rector of Christ Church, Guilford, in Connecticut. Leonard had written to Baker saying he would like to earn part of his passage by speaking, though, as he said, 'I am not one of those who always feel, "Woe is me if I do not preach the Gospel".' Baker recalls that Leonard did preach in Guilford and told something of the story of his imprisonment in Singapore:

This had a tremendous effect, but much more was the almost instant rapport which he and Mary both succeeded in making in our parish. His charm and wit and informality immediately endeared him to our New England friends. He was most interested in our family, and my wife and I both felt we could talk with Leonard and Mary as friends although we had seen so little of them for many years.

It was at Leonard's suggestion that, when they met again after the conference at Minneapolis, Baker went to Evanston where the World Council of Churches was meeting, and began the talks which ended in his being appointed as Secretary of the Overseas Council in succession to McLeod Campbell. Leonard preached in Montreal Cathedral, in New Haven and in New York. He went to Niagara Falls and found them even more impressive than he had imagined. He waited three hours in the Senate in order to listen to Senator Flanders's censure motion on Senator McCarthy, and then stayed for another four hours to hear the debate.

This was typical of the opportunities that Leonard made out of his foreign tours. The personal contacts always meant more to him than the official business, and also he liked to have time to enjoy the places and the scenes he visited. On one occasion he went to Mainz and Frankfurt with his industrial chaplain, Canon Ralph Stevens. The main purpose of the visit was to address a conference of businessmen and learn something of the German industrial situation. It was a tightly packed programme, but Leonard was determined to find time to ride on a particular Rhine Express, a journey which had nothing to do with the work in hand, and this he succeeded in doing, though not without considerable anxiety to those who were responsible for his official engagements.

It was important for Leonard to have time for his family. The years in Birmingham saw his children leaving school, going out into the world and getting married. Helen Cole-King, his daughter Susan's child, and Leonard's first grandchild, was christened by him in January 1958. Family holidays were very important to him and he liked to see the family gathered together at Bishop's Croft. His stepmother, who lived with them at Bishop's Croft for many years, and died only a few weeks after Leonard, was a much-loved member of the family group. Leonard was devoted to her, and she to him. For both Leonard and Mary the family meant a great deal, but they never regarded it as a closed group. Wherever they lived they kept open house, and they looked on the family as the basis for an extending circle of friends.

III   PORTRAIT IN A MIRROR

The Bishop

Before giving some account of the various questions and problems of the day in which Leonard became involved, this is, perhaps, the place to give a more general picture of the impression he made both as a bishop and as a man in the various fields in which he lived and worked; to look at his own theological position and the convictions on which this rested; and to see where and how he found his personal interests and pleasures outside his work.

Thousands, if not millions, of people knew Leonard by sight who had never seen him in the flesh, for they had seen him on television at the annual British Legion Festival of Remembrance at the Albert Hall. He was, indeed, an archetypal figure. Sir Oliver Leese, who was President of the Legion, writes, 'He was a magnificent figure at the Festival. He controlled the choir there with a rod of iron, and he gave tremendous dignity and fervour to the service.' This occasion was one of the high spots in the year for Leonard. He liked being a bishop in non-episcopal surroundings just as he liked being a parson in non-church surroundings. He treasured his own connection with the Durham Light Infantry in the First World War, and his close ties with those who had been prisoners-of-war in the Far East in the Second World War. The Festival was a royal occasion and a grand occasion, and Leonard was the right person to see that the part played by the churches matched in dignity and discipline what had gone before.

From the earliest days until the last service he conducted in St. Paul's Cathedral for the Order of St. Michael and St. George, shortly before he died, the testimony is the same. Here was someone who made worship meaningful and compelling. Leonard was a sacramentalist but his sacramentalism in worship was aesthetic rather than doctrinal in origin. He knew by instinct how to give dignity to words and actions. He had a magnificent voice and a keen sense of the appropriateness of language. Allan Shaw, now Dean of Bulawayo, who was for five years Leonard's Domestic Chaplain, writes:

> His way of conducting the annual rehearsal in St. Paul's for the C.M.G. Service was a perfect revelation of his dignity and courtesy. With his enormous voice, sounding out above the crowds who were sightseeing, he would call out instructions to the large and distinguished procession which he had to control, and they responded quickly and affectionately to his commands.

And speaking of Leonard as a preacher, he goes on:

> I have never heard audiences quieter than when listening to him. He certainly had the power of impressive utterance. An unmistakable presence, a great voice, and this quiet all-commanding projection of his own integrity, all combined to make him a speaker much in demand. You could hear a pin drop as he gave his Confirmation addresses.

Mr. R. E. Eason, who had been at Oxford at the same time as Leonard, and later became a master at Radley, got him to preach to the school. He recalls that for him, as for many of the boys, it was the most memorable sermon they had ever heard in the college chapel. The preparation of sermons and addresses did not come easily to Leonard and he took great pains over it. The Reverend J. P. Hickinbotham, Principal of Wycliffe Hall, remembers a visit paid by Leonard to Cranmer Hall, Durham, when he was principal there. Leonard preached in the evening in chapel, and spoke informally the next morning on the evangelical task of the Church. The sermon was on the Christian attitude to suffering which Leonard dealt with in a deeply moving way without any direct reference to his own experiences. The morning talk was full of wit, literary quotations and thought-provoking aphorisms, among which was the statement that 'There will be no great revival of religion until people once again learn to appreciate poetry.' The principal writes:

The two things which impressed me most were, first, the wide range of his personality, the simple piety and heroic witness which came out in the sermon, contrasting and yet harmonising with the wit and culture and literary allusions of the address next morning. And, second, every word of the sermon and the supposedly informal talk had obviously been carefully and meticulously prepared, although it so happened that we had had a series of visits from diocesan bishops, who had either produced what was manifestly old stuff prepared for a different audience or had talked extemporarily and badly. The fact that Leonard Birmingham had put such a great deal of work into his talks impressed the ordinands no end. On a lighter note I was much struck by the appalling old hat and flannel shirt and crumpled suit in which he arrived.

Although Leonard had this tremendous sense of occasion in all worship, in simple services just as much as on splendid cere-monial occasions, not only was he entirely free from self-importance, but he was also blessed with an impish sense of the ridiculous which poked fun at false pomp and ceremony. On one occasion a particularly High Church server had genuflected and kissed Leonard's ring. Leonard turned to his chaplain and whispered, 'His nose is cold,' without losing any of the dignity of the moment. At an ordination service in the cathedral, Leonard was bothered about the arrangements for the service.

Presumably they had not been under his control. As the pro-cession moved off from the vestry, Leonard turned to his chap-lain and remarked acidly, 'Look at those clergy rolling down the aisle.' Later in the service when he had occasion to be near the chaplain, he said in an undertone, 'So far, so good.' At the consecration of Coventry Cathedral, the Lord Mayor, who was wearing the heavy black and gold robe of his office, fainted. Everyone was frozen still, but Leonard with episcopal dignity detached himself from his fellow bishops and fetched a glass of water, which he solemnly carried before him as he would the chalice at communion. Leonard's chauffeur, Ken Darlow, recalls taking Leonard for a service on a site where a new church was to be built. As there was nowhere for Leonard to change, he robed, or as Ken put it, 'dolled himself up', in the back of the car. He carried a small wooden crook, and when Ken saw that the procession was ready he said to Leonard, 'Come on, Bo Peep, your flock is waiting for you.' In the course of the address, Leonard pointed at Ken, and said, 'If you're like the fellow sitting up there in the car, he thinks I'm Bo Peep.'

Dr. David Molesworth, a friend of Singapore days, who, after the war, went back to the leprorium near Kuala Lumpur, was asked by Leonard to build a church in the leprorium so that he could dedicate it before he left Malaya. Dr. Molesworth designed the church and the patients built it. He writes:

Before it was due to be dedicated I had a deputation to request a special graveyard for the Christians. I pointed out that the burial area was mixed to put it mildly and that during the war there had been no such nice distinctions. I was then asked if the bishop would bless the whole area. I said I felt the Chinese who shared the plot had better be consulted. This resulted in three days of gong-beating and crackers at the end of which the Chinese leaders of religion reappeared and said they thought it would be very nice if a Christian bishop blessed the area. I thanked them, and then as an afterthought, asked why, and received the answer, 'Sir, in the next world one cannot be sure who is right.' So I wrote and told Leonard this and asked if he wished to put down a box barrage or a special area. He decided to play it off the episcopal cuff. On the day there was a tremendous turn-out, bishops in full dress

134

being rare. The church was duly dedicated. Leonard, having given the final blessing, announced that we would now consecrate the graveyard and turning to me, said, 'Would you lead on, friend?' So I solemnly headed the procession till we reached the edge of the area where an assortment of mounds, stones, crosses and urns confronted us, and I indicated this was it. Very quietly he said to me, 'Definitely a box barrage', and then, without a pause, and raising his voice, went straight into the 23rd Psalm.

Dr Lilias Begg used to attend Leonard's stepmother, when she was living with the Wilsons at Bishop's Croft. Old Mrs. Wilson's maid-companion died, and the funeral service was a private family affair in the bishop's chapel. Dr. Begg had a niece staying with her at the time who said that she had never been to a funeral and was frightened of them. Leonard took the service, and the girl said afterwards to her aunt, 'I shall never be afraid of a funeral again. I think it was a lovely party.'

In ways like these Leonard made the services he took inspiring, helpful and homely, and this was a gift which never deserted him. It was in keeping with this that what he thought was unnecessary fuss and pomposity in the ordering of worship made him angry, and sometimes provoked acid comment. On one occasion the consecration of a new church on a Saturday was followed the next day by a choral parish communion at which Leonard was going to celebrate. In the vestry, the vicar was explaining to Leonard their 'use'. He said, 'We say the Preparation before the altar when we get into our places.' Leonard replied, 'I do my preparation at home; we won't do it again.' On another occasion on a visit to a church with a strong High Church tradition, a layman, who was acting as master of the ceremonies, said to Leonard, 'You won't mind if I put you right on our procedure?' To which Leonard answered, 'Not a bit, if you don't mind my telling you when I've had enough.'

The magnificent coped figure who appeared on the television

screen every Remembrance Festival and the shabby-suited figure in an appalling old hat who went to speak to the ordinands at Cranmer Hall hid the same man. When Bishop David Porter, formerly Bishop of Aston, and Bishop Sinker were installed as canons of the cathedral, the Lord Mayor gave a reception, and the two men walked across to it in their purple cassocks. Leonard was annoyed and said, 'You look like a couple of old women.' But when all three bishops happened to be at a service together, Leonard would not allow the others to wear their mitres. He seemed to regard it as a crown, and there was only one king.

It will be recalled that, many years before, when Leonard had gone to Singapore to spy out the land, after he had been appointed bishop, but before he was consecrated, he attended matins in the cathedral wearing a tie, and yet John Hayter was taken to task for omitting any special prayer for the bishop-elect, though he may well have thought that coming so dressed Leonard wished to remain incognito. It is possible that Leonard's ambivalent attitude to clerical dress was an unconscious reaction to his ambivalent love–hate relationship with the Church, which someone described as being of Bairnsfather's drawing, *If Yer Know of a Better 'Ole, Go To It*. In the diocese he appeared as often in a tie as in a clerical collar. On one occasion when he was setting off to the Garden Party at Buckingham Palace, Bishop Porter said he ought to be wearing gaiters, to which Leonard replied, 'The Queen doesn't like gaiters.' Whether that was true or not, it was a fact that the archbishop took quite a line about them. At a Bishops' Meeting at Lambeth, Fisher sent a note to Leonard, asking him to come to see him the next day at 11 a.m. To do this Leonard had to alter an engagement already made. When he got to Lambeth, he was kept waiting half an hour before being shown into Fisher's study. Fisher walked up and down saying, 'Now what was it I wanted to see you about?' After a pause he went on, 'O yes, I remember. I wanted to tell you that when you come to Bishops' Meetings, I hope you will come properly dressed.' This was not the only occasion Leonard was taken to task for not wearing gaiters. However, there was a happy sequel to these admonitions, for when Leonard was ill in St. Thomas's Hospital, Fisher came to visit him wearing trousers, and said, 'Leonard, I have put these on specially for you.' But the tide was turning and Leonard was on the winning side in this sartorial battle. A stalwart of the old tradition saw Leonard at a Bishops' Meeting taking off his coat preparatory to removing a jersey he was wearing, and remarked in a loud voice, 'Bishops no longer come in proper dress, and now they are beginning to take off their coats.'

The Man

In a Press interview in 1963 under the title *What Birmingham Means to Me*, Leonard said:

> The well-being of the individual is the supreme considera-
> tion. I cannot separate my thoughts and reflections on Birm-
> ingham, and what it means to me, from the numerous people
> in all walks of life, with whom I come into daily contact. I am
> humble and glad to have made friends of so many of them.
> They reassure me for our city's well-being and future, for I
> am a great believer in the basic soundness and goodness of the
> majority of ordinary people.

Bishop Porter said of Leonard, 'To me his outstanding characteristic was his ability to attract affection from an amazingly wide acquaintance, a large proportion of whom became his friends.'

Something has already been said of this quality of humanity which all through his life marked Leonard's personal relationships. It is certain that it played a large part in his years as Bishop of Birmingham, and it is important to look at this in relation to the clergy and laity of the diocese, both individually and in groups, and in relation to individuals and groups outside the diocese, including his fellow bishops.

High office and large responsibilities sometimes have a corroding effect on a man's capacity for human friendship. It is one of the corruptions of power, and it is a corruption which can be observed in the life of clerics as much as in those who move in what some would think of as more worldly circumstances. Charles Raven was once having lunch with a friend who had just been made a bishop. The friend said, 'It's sad to think, Charles, that in the future we shall not be able to meet like this as equals.' It is hard to imagine anyone saying this, though some by their changed attitude, would appear, consciously or unconsciously, to think it. Leonard could never for a moment have thought like that. He never forgot his friends. The Reverend Oliver Fielding Clarke writes, 'I got to know him at Oxford in 1919. Leonard, or Tubby as we always called him, impressed me at once by his cheerfulness and the feeling he gave you of sheer goodness.' The two friends met again, nearly forty years later, at the Modern Churchmen's Conference. Fielding Clarke writes:

Tubby knew me at once, and remembered also that I was usually known as Bernard, and talked about common friends of Oxford days. I was frankly just amazed by his memory for people belonging to a bygone age, when you think of all the thousands of people he must have met over the years. And it was not just a good memory; it was genuine human and Christian concern for others that struck me so forcibly. Tubby in 1958 at the conference seemed to me just like the Tubby of Oxford days.

This ministry of friendship and care, which was so marked a feature of Leonard's life, stood him in good stead when he first arrived in Birmingham. The diocese needed to be brought together, and this he did. The 'rebels', who were left from Barnes's day, were brought inside the circle, and the diocese was quick to respond to the family atmosphere which Leonard created. The clergy were not long in realising that here was someone who was readily accessible and would spare no time or thought to help them where he could. He got on well with the younger clergy, particularly the more difficult ones. Perhaps he saw in some of them himself at an earlier age. No one who came to him with a personal problem went away without his horizon being enlarged. When he called men in to discuss a new job with them, he would never try to persuade them to accept the post, even if he felt strongly that the man was the right person for it. He would put the pros and cons and leave the individual completely free. 'I never press men,' he said. This too, was part of his innate respect for the individual. The person was more important than the job, any job. Like everybody else, he had his blind spots, and in a few cases allowed his dislike of a man's theology, or what he thought was his theology, to be a barrier to a better human understanding. There were one or two Anglo–Catholics of whom this was true, and at the other end, speaking of Conservative–Evangelicals, he sometimes quoted with approval Barnes's aphorism, 'An evangelical not by conviction but by lethargy.' It is strange that both of them should have joined in a judgment which in nine cases out of ten is so obviously untrue. The Conservative–Evangelical may sometimes be narrow in his views but he holds them with conviction, and his attitude is the reverse of lethargic.

It was on the individual plane that Leonard was at his best with the clergy. In larger clerical or official gatherings he was less at ease, though outstanding exceptions were the three-yearly clergy meetings at Swanwick or elsewhere. Here, he felt he was on holiday with his clergy, and Leonard's holiday spirit was always full of life and humour. But at Diocesan Conferences, committees, meetings of his senior staff and such gatherings, Leonard was less sure of himself. He very much enjoyed visiting parishes, preaching and meeting the people, but he was never happy at the cathedral. It is possible that some people are good at meeting and others good at meetings, and never the twain shall meet. In Leonard's case it would be true to say that he was not good at formal meetings. At informal ones he was often the life and soul of the party. On formal occasions, he was apt to be on his guard. He was apprehensive of people whom he thought were more quick-witted than himself. As a chairman he found it very difficult to take criticism, and he was not above using his position to come down heavily on speakers who were taking a line of their own which was different from his. In this way he could be very ruthless, and there were some who kept quiet at Diocesan Conferences because they did not feel called upon to endure this kind of treatment in public.

Leonard appointed a high-powered commission to make recommendations with regard to the church situation in the centre of the city, where, as a result of the bombing and the movement of population, drastic reorganisation was needed. But he took no notice of their report and the general reaction of those who had done the work was, 'What's the good of giving advice if he takes no notice of it?' On one occasion at a meeting of his senior staff, he banged on the table, shouted at the offender, 'You're calling me a liar,' and walked out of the room. But he did not harbour rancour. He was aware of his weaknesses. Paul Burrough, now Bishop of Mashonaland, who worked closely and in deep friendship with Leonard as his Chaplain to Overseas Peoples, recalls:

I remember one occasion when I was put up at the Diocesan Conference to oppose him very strongly on a matter with which he was concerned. He was somewhat hurt and angry at the time, and said that he hoped I would withdraw the amendment on the topic under debate, and when the subject had been well aired, I did ask for the amendment to be withdrawn. This was on a Thursday night, and the next morning, being a Friday, I was at his house early for the Eucharist which he held for the senior staff each week in the private chapel. He looked at me and merely said, 'Am I forgiven?' This was no false modesty. He didn't like having to cross a person, but he was always prepared to do so in the honest tussle of minds which was for him one of the joys of life as well as its responsibility.

Leonard always trusted people, and though he was bitter when he thought they had let him down, he never gave up the principle. He enjoyed winning a row, and always tried to come back at his opponent if he was losing. Sometimes he found it difficult to bury the hatchet, but he believed so strongly in the idea of reconciliation, that he was never really at ease while the estrangement lasted. This is, after all, a common feature in the complexity of human relationships. Men assert most passionately their belief in the things which they find the hardest to practise. There was, too, a streak of laziness in Leonard's make-up. This was partly why he avoided, whenever he could, serving on commissions and committees. But partly, also, it was his instinct that he must not become too involved in machinery if he was to do the human job which he really believed in. This was one reason why he so often came home depressed from Bishops' Meetings, Convocation, and the Church Assembly. So much of their discussion and debate seemed to him too far removed from the real pastoral work of the Church, and even when this was its concern, too narrowly conceived.

Most of his fellow bishops thought that the contribution Leonard made was a valuable one. He did not speak a great deal, but when he did, it was always to the point. In Bishops' Meetings he had a great gift of asking the awkward questions which everyone was thinking, but nobody would voice. On one occasion, they had spent a whole morning discussing whether the wine for Communion should be fermented. Leonard said, 'I have only one thing to say, let's put in the adjective "good" and scrap the rest.' He had an independent mind which was impatient of ecclesiasticism. In the Church Assembly he would often support a minority view just to make sure that it had a fair hearing. When he really fought for something, he carried a great deal of weight. He always stood on the side of proposals which were liberal in spirit. He wanted doors opened. Although he was always loyal to the decisions when they were made, he was sad, and sometimes bitter, when they seemed to him narrow and rigoristic rather than open-ended and charitable. At Bishops' Meetings he never said anything in a way that would hurt or offend anyone. He felt much more sure of himself in meetings where he did not carry the responsibility of being in the chair.

In January 1960, Leonard had to pay a visit to hospital for treatment of a skin trouble partly due to varicose veins. Two years before, when the trouble had first occurred, he had written to the archbishop asking to be excused from the Bishops' Meetings. He said in this letter, 'The war years in Singapore did some damage which has just come to light. Perhaps the extra number of times I wore gaiters at the Lambeth Conference has contributed. I am sorry to spoil my record of one hundred per cent attendance.' Leonard must have written in the same vein two years later, because Fisher replied:

I am sorry, and only hope that with medical aid you will cast 'it' off speedily and thoroughly. We shall miss you greatly. You do not know how much I rely on you as a kind of thermometer to show how near we are to sanity and common sense on each question as it arises. I do hope you will be all right for Convocation.

He added in his own handwriting, 'I read your letter to the bishops who received it with sympathy and hilarity!'

If sometimes they found Leonard unpredictable, his fellow bishops on the bench had a great affection for him as a man, and considerable respect for his practical wisdom and judgment. In the secret places of the Upper House, the bishops have their own robing room, each with his own cupboard, which resembles the cupboards that used to be provided for members' golf-bags at the local club. Leonard's happened to be detached from the rest in a cubby-hole round the corner. Even that seems symbolic

When Leonard was in the House of Lords for the last time, he took two of his fellow bishops aside, and, laying his hand with great dignity on the head of the one who was the newcomer, said, 'I hereby induct you into this locker with all its appurtenances.'

In the last preface to *Crockford*, that Private Eye of the Church of England which has delighted the off-beat clergy for many years, the writer said of Leonard, 'He was one of the most remarkable men to occupy an English see in recent years. Not a man of any great intellectual attainments, he was nevertheless of great courage and spiritual strength.' The editorial comment in *The Modern Churchman* which quoted this, added, 'Unless the system allows for the appointment in the future of such men, the Church will suffer great loss.' There will be few among those who saw Leonard at work in the higher councils of the Church who will disagree with this comment.

Leonard had a love-hate relationship with the establishment. That was why he felt so much freer, and was more spontaneous, when he was outside it. Whenever he could, he went to Twickenham for the university rugger match, and he used to enjoy the big cricket games both at Edgbaston and Lord's. He was a member of the Warwickshire County Cricket Club and Sir Oliver Leese, its President, writes of Leonard's visits, 'We always welcomed him to our V.I.P. luncheons, but he often preferred to watch the cricket quietly and unobtrusively from places in the pavilion where we had little opportunity to know if he was on the ground.' Michael Clarke, formerly Provost of Birmingham describes one visit to Twickenham, 'He was wearing a rough Scotch tweed suit and the tie of some Oxford club, and was in holiday spirits. So absorbed was he that his limbs twitched at various movements on the field, like a dog's as he dreams over the hunt. "Being a good fly-half," he said, "places you in a class way above bishops and provosts." '

He was always more at home in non-church gatherings. He was a welcome guest backstage at Birmingham theatres at

Christmas time when he came to wish the pantomime cast good luck. He never lost his love and loyalty for the north country, and the garden parties at Bishop's Croft for the local branch of the Northumberland and Durham Association, of which he was President, were occasions which he loved. He was a welcome speaker at rotary and service clubs. These were the kind of audiences he found it easiest to get alongside. He went to give a talk to some apprentices in Birmingham, and started by saying, 'Some of you may have noticed that the number of my car is SOB 1; that does not stand for what you think it does, it stands for Shepherd of Birmingham.' Sometimes Leonard's sense of humour changed the atmosphere of a sticky meeting. He went to one which he was afraid was not going to get off the ground, so he began with a story which was quite irrelevant to the matter in hand. When Vicar of Roker he had acted as hospital chaplain, and one day he went into a ward to find out how many Anglicans there were who would like to take Communion the following Sunday. He asked a patient, 'Are you C. of E?' The man was deaf, and he had to repeat the question louder and louder several times until the man answered, 'No, strangulated hernia.' This brought the house down and completely changed the atmosphere of the meeting.

But Leonard's gift of getting alongside people did not spring from an easy-going bonhomie. He was not easy-going either with himself or with other people. For all his apt wit, and sometimes caustic comment, he was quick to sense people's deeper needs, whether they were old or young. At a schoolboy conference a boy said to him, 'I find it very difficult to say my prayers, sir.' Leonard answered, 'Do you? So do I. I can't pray for long at all.' Dr. Begg had a case of a boy of fourteen whose condition was very difficult to diagnose. He was not an epileptic, but he sometimes behaved like one. She happened to see Leonard and told him about the boy. She said that the boy behaved as though he was possessed by an evil spirit. The next day Leonard rang her up and asked if the boy's parents would like him to go and

144

see him. He went, and shortly afterwards the boy said to Dr. Begg, 'That was a very decent chap you sent to see me the other night.'

The Reverend Christopher Hall, a son of Bishop Hall, recalls how Leonard and Mary drove eighty miles to be with the family at his brother's funeral. 'His quite unexpected presence gave my sister and myself tremendous encouragement; like the strong arm of a life-saver to a swimmer in difficulties.' Gilbert Baker, Bishop of Hong Kong, speaks for many when he writes:

> Everywhere Leonard went he brought with him a friendly, genial approach, and with it a genuine concern for people as people; and as they came to know him more and more people understood that despite of, or because of, his distaste for pious language or religious attitudes, here was a man of God to whom Christ was a reality assured and made known in the experience of suffering and in the victory that came out of it.

A foreman who had been in charge of the building of a new vicarage was invited to be present at the party on the occasion of it being blessed. 'The Bishop of Birmingham,' he said. 'I once shook hands with him. Didn't wash it for a week.' A television producer who had worked with more than one bishop, remarked, 'The Bishop of —— was the bishop of the Church people. This man is bishop of us all.' A Birmingham taxi-driver said to Michael Parker, 'I see we're losing the bishop. Ah, he'll be a hard man to follow.'

Two of the clergy in Smethwick started an Anglican club for the Smethwick deanery. Leonard and Mary went to the inaugural meeting which was held in the Londonderry Inn. *The Birmingham Mail* reported this with a picture of Leonard and three of the clergy with glasses of beer in their hands. In wishing the club success Leonard said, 'I think it is a very good thing to meet in a pub. For Anglicans to meet across parochial boundaries is better, and to have fellowship with one another is best of all. I hope the club grows, not just to keep people

together, but because you like meeting each other.' Of course
there were those who disapproved, but the truth is that Leonard
had a sure touch in this kind of matter. He knew what he was
about, and his words and actions on such occasions were rooted
in his conviction that people were lovable in themselves and
friendship could surmount all artificial human barriers.
Courtesy, consideration, and large-heartedness were the hall-
mark of his relationships, and there is no doubt that Leonard
believed that these virtues could only be his as he shared in the
'meekness and gentleness' of Christ.

Beliefs and Convictions

Leonard was not an academic theologian, but he was fully able
to find his way about in the subject so that he understood the
theological issues behind the human, social and ecclesiastical
questions and problems of the day. His own religious outlook
sprang from three roots; his evangelical upbringing; his discovery of the freedoms of a liberal spirit, which he began to
learn under F. R. Barry and Mervyn Haig at Knutsford, and
continued to find under Streeter's influence at Oxford; and his
love of poetry which gave him an imaginative understanding of
symbolism and imagery. It was the combination of these three,
coupled with a splendid voice and sense of words, that made his
sermons memorable.

There is no doubt that Leonard believed the Christian Gospel
to be 'the power of God unto salvation'. He wrote:

Evangelism is difficult work and therefore is in danger of being
neglected. It is difficult because it is not clearly defined. It will
make for clearness of thought and effectiveness of action if
evangelistic work is distinguished from, though it cannot be
separated from, three other aspects of the Church's work.
First, it is not the same as the intellectual presentation of the
Christian faith as the Christian answer to the intellectual
problem of today. Men have to be moved to do much more
than to give intellectual adherence to the Christian position.

146

Second, it is not the same as the application of Christian principles to social and international questions. People must be taught to surrender to Christ and His Kingdom and not merely to be won over to a 'social reform' movement. Third, it is not the same as a movement for the deepening of the spiritual life of those who are already members of the Church. All these three things are important, but are not themselves evangelism. The evangelistic work of the Church is the impinging upon an unconverted, half-converted, or nominally Christian world, of the Gospel; the winning of men and women to a real fellowship with Christ.

For Leonard this belief in evangelism was strengthened, not emasculated, by the spirit of free inquiry and a liberal interpretation of the fundamental facts of the Christian faith. 'You shall know the truth, and the truth shall make you free' was one of his favourite texts. He wrote:

For many people today the essential part of knowing and learning and education seems to be the power to give right answers to questions. It is counted high praise of a man to say, 'He knows all the answers.' But surely it is as important, if not more important, to ask the right questions. The world needs more men and women who have the kind of mind that knows what are the right questions to ask of themselves and their environment.

And in a B.B.C. interview, he said:

I haven't got the kind of faith that is ready-made. I've had to fight for it. I've always been questioning. I've questioned the creeds; I've questioned the Bible; I've questioned the Establishment; I've questioned the way the Church works; and I'm going on questioning all my life, I hope, because I hope to find that the Holy Spirit will lead me to a deeper understanding of what God really wants in this world.

When Leonard accepted the position of President of the Modern Churchmen's Union, that body was in need of some kind of rescue operation. It was regarded by many as just iconoclastic and irrelevant. Leonard gave it dignity and was largely responsible for giving the movement a wider basis. He had always been a liberal in outlook, but it was good for the Modern Churchmen's Union to have as its President one whose faith was essentially simple. It was also good for the Church at large to see that a modern churchman could go through the Changi ordeal by and for his faith.

Following the Modern Churchmen's Conference in 1964, *The Times* had a leader under the title *Honest or Not*, which raised the question of the sincerity of clergy in the Church of England reciting creeds which contained doctrines about which they expressed doubts. To this Leonard replied in a letter to *The Times* in which he said:

> This charge has been levelled against some clergy for over two hundred years. It is without foundation but based on assumptions about Christianity and about our Church which are contrary to the letter and spirit of the New Testament, of our own Prayer Book and of our history as a Christian nation. The primary assumption is that Christianity was once and fully delivered in unalterable formularies; it is assumed further that these formularies are only fully to be found in our Church and its Prayer Book; and it is therefore naturally the business of the clergy of that Church only to expound and defend these formularies. It is assumed to be of no account that with time some of these formularies become difficult to understand, and some impossible to accept.
>
> When a clergyman recites a form of words more than sixteen centuries old he commits himself to its general intention. He is not supposed to be committing himself to a literal affirmation of each individual statement, such as would be expected in a personal affidavit. Some clauses of our creeds,

such as 'sitting on the right hand of God', were from the beginning symbolic. Words like 'descended' and 'ascended', relics of a pre-Copernican universe, are now generally accepted as symbolical. It is dishonest to pretend that the 'faithful remnant' to which you refer accept them literally. You are right to be anxious lest restatement strays from the fundamentals of the faith when so many more ask so many new questions, but the Church of England has already taken care of this. After fifteen years of study, in 1938, a doctrinal commission reported to the Archbishops of Canterbury and York. It did not say what were the beliefs of the Church of England, but it did suggest within what limits of tolerance many of these beliefs might be held, and indicated that some could be discarded without detriment to what was fundamental. It is quite possible to accept wholeheartedly the reality of Our Lord's Incarnation without being committed to a belief in the Virgin Birth. I should doubt if in the past twenty-five years any member of the Modern Churchmen's Union, clerical or lay, has often gone beyond the limits of this report in stating what he believed.

Leonard told a friend whom he had known since Coventry days, 'If you want to know what Christianity is about, read St. Mark's Gospel.' It may not be the whole truth but one could go a very long way without getting any truer or better advice.

The letter to *The Times* fairly represents Leonard's liberal approach to Christian doctrine, and he found no difficulty in reconciling this with his belief in the evangelistic power of the Christian faith. In this he was helped by his understanding of poetic imagery and symbolism. It would be true to say that he found the truth of sacramentalism equally in the splendour of natural beauty, in the language of poetry, and in the rites of the Church. He wrote in the diocesan leaflet of a Whitsuntide holiday when he had journeyed through the byways and lanes of Herefordshire and Gloucestershire:

I would agree that there are in other lands more majestic scenes of rugged cliffs and snow-topped mountains than can be seen in England, but for homely restful beauty and joy, the English countryside is the fairest scenery on earth I know. And on Whit Monday I feasted my eyes on it; the sweet rise and fall of rolling woods, the shimmering lines of rolling downs, the dreamy distances of brooding hills on the borderland of Wales. There was breeze enough to move the fields of young springing corn, and so to change the pattern of the shades of green as the wind swept along the hillside. The splendour of spreading beech trees and the shadows of the tufted elms all wove their spell of beauty. Patient cows stood beside the silent pools, and half-grown lambs scampered away to frolic or to seek security beside their mothers. The sun's transforming power was everywhere. Its warmth was welcome enough, but the magic of its light transformed the scene. It was easy to understand the ancient religion of sun worshippers, but more comforting to know the Lord and Giver of Light and Life and the Light of the World. The perception of beauty brings an inner content; and as we learn to recognise beauty in simple and commonplace things, we begin to gain insight into the ordering of a world whose Creator and Perfecter is Beauty, Truth and Goodness.

In an article entitled *Religious Education in State Schools*, which Leonard wrote for *The Birmingham Teachers' Journal*, he said:

By Christian humanism I mean the love of all things human in art and science and literature, together with a recognition that beyond man there is a Creator and Judge before whom he stands responsible, and that beyond this temporal existence there is eternal life. Christian humanism enables men and women to have a truly comprehensive idea of nature. Nature includes all the phenomena that God has made: planets, plants, animals, birds, and man both in his affinity to the inanimate world with which he is bound up, and in his affinity to his Creator, with the capacity for goodness and love which this involves. The study of nature includes all this.

Indeed this should be implicit in all study, and that surely is one interpretation of religious education.

If we teach science, let us take a large view of it. What does it include? The understanding of the visible world; not only the data which the mechanistic sciences deal with, but all the data of order and beauty in the world, that is to say nature in its older and comprehensive meaning. Our teaching will be touching only a fragment of this, but we can do it in such a way as not only to impart knowledge, but to invoke awe and wonder. In this way our work will have some relation to the daily act of worship.

To all the social, international, and ecclesiastical questions and problems which presented themselves while Leonard was Bishop of Birmingham he brought an evangelical and liberal Christian faith and judgment, and he found a steadying influence to his involvement in them in his much-loved Keats,

> Beauty is truth, truth beauty—that is all
> Ye know on earth, and all ye need to know.

His faith was robust, without being hearty; tolerant without being easy-going. He had a firm grasp of fundamentals and was impatient of frills. He made no claim to originality, but he had a fresh and attractive way of expressing the truths which were dear to him. In a sermon in Westminster Abbey in 1967 on the occasion of the Fiftieth Jubilee Celebration of the Women's Services, speaking of the failure of service being a failure in ourselves, he said:

Everyman's fate is himself. So elemental is this fact that one might expect people to determine resolutely to take charge of their own lives and characters, but the reverse seems to be true. We all have ways of dodging the issue.

We trust in our fortunate circumstances and privileges rather than in ourselves, like the lady in one of Walter Scott's novels who 'relied upon a fine set of china to heighten the flavour of indifferent tea'. Some think they can bluff through life by having possessions, but there is a vast difference between possession and ownership. I don't possess any land, but no one can take the landscape from me. Possession is having a library of books you never read. Ownership is saying with Fenelon, 'If all the crowns of Europe were laid at my feet in exchange for my love of reading, I would spurn them all.' Possession is having a house; ownership is having a home . . . Nor can we bluff through life by attempts to be useful. The choicest gift that anyone can give to his friends is himself at his best. Most people are willing to give anything rather than that . . . How seldom do we see examples of that most excellent gift of gracious giving of true friendship and companionship; for so many of us have so little to give.

When he spoke of suffering, he was always concerned to emphasise the possibility of its becoming an enrichment of life.

Active, willing, conscious acceptance of our share in the tragedy of life, this is something positive and creative. In turning such experience to creative use we have first to understand the laws under which these elemental things like pain operate. If you are prepared to face pain in this way, accepting it and believing that it can be turned to practical use, you make a strange discovery. Not only do you find out the way to bear it so that it hurts you less; you know that in its willing acceptance there lie ways of growth in personality, sympathy and enrichment of life which before you never expected . . . There remains the most difficult problem of all; how are we to understand the suffering of others and especially of those we love, whose pain we can only watch and not alleviate? There are times when we are called to watch great suffering, crushing bereavement, overwhelming calamity, and when all our theories about suffering and its uses simply shrivel up, and if we try to put them into words it sounds hollow and a mockery.

Then most of all we need to learn to conquer by accepting. It may be given to us by an act of penetrating sympathy to enter into their suffering and in a sense accept it for them, and so help them, perhaps only later, to make their own acceptance. More even than this, we ought to remind ourselves that God feels this pain as much, indeed more than we do, because of His more perfect sympathy.

This conviction about the creative possibility of suffering rightly accepted came out of his own experience. With it went an equally strong belief in personal immortality. In his last message to the diocesan leaflet he wrote of this as one of the central truths for him.

A third conviction which has grown stronger with the years, but which is, to my regret, not universally held even by those who call themselves Christians, is that I believe in the life of the world to come. Our citizenship is in heaven as well as on earth. I am sceptical of some of the traditional images of the life after death, but of the fact of it I have no doubt. Here, of course, I cannot speak from experience, but I hope I will be included in the benediction, 'Blessed are those who have not seen and yet have believed.' To me the conviction of the life of the world to come follows naturally from the character of God.

If anyone asked Leonard how many children he had, he always answered, 'We have five; one is no longer with us.' His convictions were simple, but they had been hardly won. Once, when talking to an old friend, he said that he was worried about his doubts, and then added, after a pause, 'You mustn't think that at bottom I have any doubts at all. I haven't.' And this was the impression he left on those who knew him best. Bishop Burrough writes:

Although he was often thought to be a Modernist bishop, who was critical of some aspects of Church doctrine, I would say that the most powerful effect he had on me was one of absolute assurance of the fundamental Christian verities. I have often used his famous phrase from prison-camp days, 'The Resurrection has the last word,' and no one could doubt that he believed this to be so, and that in the most stormy days of his life.

As we have seen, Leonard used the time he had in Singapore before he was interned to strengthen the ties with other churches and to promote Church unity, and when he returned again in 1947, this continued to be one of his main concerns. In Birmingham, he always had good relationships with the Roman Catholic Church and with the Free Churches, both personal and official. When Archbishop Grimshaw was dying in hospital, Leonard went to see him, as he also went to see Leslie Tizzard, the Minister at Carr's Lane in similar circumstances. Dr. Dwyer, the present Archbishop of Birmingham, writes:

We had friendly contact from the first and he would send his chaplains for youth work and the Church Army to see me and discuss how we might co-operate. We shared the platform in January 1966 in Birmingham Town Hall at a meeting during the Week of Prayer for Unity among Christians. This was the first time it had happened in Birmingham (I mean the sharing). Our theological positions were in many respects very different, but I was always struck by his evident personal piety, his devotion to Christ Our Lord and his sense of prayer. We also shared the same kind of sense of humour. When I was invited to speak at his farewell meeting in the Town Hall

I quoted some Latin tag or other, and he took an impish delight in capping it with half a dozen lines of Virgil! I believe he was a member of the Modern Churchmen's Union, but on the occasions when I heard him speak on fundamental questions I was struck by the way he spoke in line with the main tradition of Christian thought, notably in a paper he read on the problem of suffering. It was an annual foundation lecture in the School of Medicine here. I even heard him say when we returned to the vestry after I had been attending vespers, and I think preaching, in S. Martin's in the Bullring, 'Eternal rest give to them O Lord and let perpetual light shine upon them: May they rest in peace,' which wasn't bad going for a modern churchman, though of course it might have been ecumenism. But he was too straight to put on an act.

When the scheme for reunion with the Methodist Church was turned down by the Church Assembly, Leonard went to communion the following Sunday morning at Northfield Methodist Church and made it known that he was doing so.

Out of School

Men of deep conviction often find their pleasure in simple things. This was true of Leonard. He loved parties, and especially children's parties; he loved the countryside, and to explore the byways. He loved his birthday and opening his cards and presents. He was always a bad letter-writer, but if his children were away from him, they could be certain of getting a letter on their birthday. He remembered the birthdays of the older generation in his family and the following letter to his aunt, Miss Wilson, written from Blundell House, Tiverton, on May 26th, 1957, is typical:

My dear Auntie May,

Herewith my outward and visible sign that I will be thinking and praying for you tomorrow that you may have many happy returns of the day: with a body free from pain, a mind free from worry and a soul at peace.

Years and years ago you wrote of 'Heartsease'. May you have it now. I've been preaching at this school this morning and return to Birmingham this afternoon. Please give my love to May and Leslie and my kind remembrances to such friends at Witton as are still about. I hope it won't be long before I see you. With love, Len.

In April 1968, after his visit to Biafra, he wrote to his eldest son, Timothy, who was in South America with his family, to give him an account of the expedition, and began as follows:

My dear Tim,

I have just written the first page of this letter on blotting paper, thinking it was the first page of a new pad, so I have to start again. I know it is a long time since I wrote to you but this does not argue any lack of affection on my part. On the contrary my conscience is so disturbed that you and the family are in my thoughts three or four times a day. I was sorry especially that you didn't get a birthday letter from me. But, having missed my annual letter, you will be surprised to get an extra or a substitute.

He was at his happiest with his family and when they could be on holiday together. He loved to plan the routes they would take whether by train or car. All his life he had a passion for trains, and had he been a guest on *Desert Island Discs*, he would have wanted on his island, after the Bible and Shakespeare, the continental Bradshaw. In September 1968, he paid a visit to his brother Leslie, who was then Rector of Winterbourne Strickland in Dorset, and on arrival home he wrote to describe his journey:

My journey home when I left you at Salisbury was interesting and frustrating. We made good progress, up to time, till within three miles of Basingstoke. We were then halted because part of the line was blocked because of a fallen embankment which meant single line working. Eventually we arrived at Basingstoke fifty minutes late. I jumped out quickly with luggage, and asked hopefully if the York train had gone. 'Yes, it has,' said the official. 'Then what do I do to get to Birmingham?' says I. 'You'd best go to Reading General,' says he. 'How?' says I. 'Back in the train you just got out of.' So I hopped back quickly and set off in the stopping train, but it stopped at more than stations, and when I popped my head out when the signal was red, and found a plateman standing, I asked what the hold up was this time. I was told the York train in front was having a bit of bother. I asked if there was any chance of it waiting for us at Reading. He said there might be as, 'They has to change engines there.' As our little train came into Reading, I saw the York ready to pull out. I gave a mighty shout to wait, and did the hundred yards through the tunnels and just caught it. I got my breath back before we got to Banbury, and arrived home just less than an hour late, an exciting finish to a marvellous though less strenuous weekend, for which I thank you very much.

Leonard had all the railway timetables and knew many of the connections without looking them up. Sometimes he made mistakes, and then it was a matter of honour to retrieve the position. His chauffeur, Ken Darlow, recalls how once he got into the wrong train at Paddington, and found himself travelling to Wales instead of Birmingham. However, he realised he could catch a connection at Bristol for Worcester, and he got a porter at a station they passed through to send a telegram to Ken telling him to meet him at Worcester. His ability to retrieve the situation fully compensated him for his initial mistake.

When travelling by car, Leonard liked to take short cuts through the back streets of cities and towns, and for a long journey, when there was time, or he was on holiday, he would get out the maps and plan a route which kept to the B roads for as much of the time as possible. But he was also enthusiastic about the motorways, and did his best to get on to them as soon as they were opened. Shortly after the M1 was opened, he was driving along it with Ken sitting beside him. He asked about a combination in front of them, when they were doing ninety miles an hour, 'What's that in front?' To which Ken replied, 'If you can't see for yourself, I'm getting out.'

During the 1958 Lambeth Conference, Leonard and Greer stayed at a country inn in the Cotswolds, which Leonard had discovered. They neither of them fancied being in close proximity to their fellow bishops all the time. They travelled up each day to Marylebone with R. O. Hall, who had a house near by. In the evenings they would go for walks and drives in the Cotswolds. As usual Leonard knew all the side roads, and Greer remembers driving slowly along one of them in the evening when there was a crowd of sparrows in the middle of the road. Leonard drove very slowly, blowing his horn, until the sparrows were safely out of the way.

At the end of one of the Swedish conferences which Leonard attended, he went with Bishop and Mrs. Hunter on a holiday in Norway, Leonard driving their car with great skill and dash. On one occasion they stopped on a mountainous road, which ran by the edge of a steep precipice. Leonard put his head out of the window, peered over the edge, and said, 'It's all right, there's an inch to spare.' Much of the zest for life which Leonard enjoyed arose out of situations of all kinds where there was only an inch to spare.

IV   BRICKS AND MORTAR

From the first Leonard realised that the growth of Birmingham laid an enormous task on the diocese. They were short of men and they were short of buildings. The number of clergy was smaller than at the end of Gore's time, while, of course, the population had grown enormously. Nothing could be done without money, and it soon became clear to Leonard that he was faced with raising a large sum. When he arrived in the diocese, Michael Clarke was Provost of the Cathedral and Bryan Green was Rector of Birmingham. Harvie Clark was Archdeacon of Birmingham and Michael Parker Archdeacon of Aston. Leonard petitioned the Crown for a suffragan bishop, and Parker was appointed as the first Bishop of Aston. Max Dunlop was invited by Leonard to take over the archdeaconry of Aston, and, after some hesitation, agreed to do so. Dunlop had gone to Manchester at Greer's suggestion about the same time as Leonard became dean. There he had worked as director of the Diocesan Education Committee. He and Leonard had been friends for many years, and the Wilsons had left their younger children with the Dunlops when they returned to Singapore in 1948. In June 1954, Dunlop wrote to Leonard:

If you should still think fit to ask me to consider becoming one of your archdeacons, I should be glad to do so. I have been, and still am in some degree, apprehensive, not of any consequences to our personal relations, which have survived sundry vicissitudes, but of the general effect of my inevitable way of handling the kind of situation you sketched. It requires not a log, but a stork; not only 'a chief staff officer', which I should try to be, but an administrative officer, who as one of a team, would yet have his own authority and be expected to give a lead. It will require in the early years mainly impersonal handling and the application of agreed principles. I have found that the first reaction of my fellow clergy to such an approach is one of misunderstanding, some resentment, and even hostility. Theirs is primarily a personal job. I do not abound with enthusiasm, at my advanced and greying years, at the prospect of earning a reputation for bloody-mindedness from one's bishop down. Hence chiefly my long hesitation. But your talk with me at Feathers' went far to allay my doubts. I believe you will understand and approve of what I

159

am getting at: and eventually, when the house is built and the noise done, the clergy may like working in it because I should hope they would regard it as their own. But your doubts may be increased. I am most uncertain still if you are contemplating the right step. I should be quite happy if you wished to think again and to let me hear much later on.

Greer had been against the partnership. He knew them both well, and he did not think it would work. In one sense he was wrong, in another he was right. The tragedy was that the job was done, and well done, but the cost was an estrangement between two old friends, and, in the end, an almost complete breakdown of any personal communication between them. There were faults on both sides. A friend saw Max in hospital, shortly before he died. His breathing was difficult but that did not prevent him denouncing in forthright language an injustice which he supposed had been done to this friend by the establishment. Then, as always, behind that battling voice and spirit there was a gentle, imaginative concern for others. Only a few months earlier, when the same friend's grandson of three had been killed in a motor accident in Uganda, Max had offered to pay out of his very slendour resources the air fares to Uganda for him and his wife.

Up to within a few months before he died, Leonard was still unhappy in his mind about his relations with Max. He had not come to terms with the breakdown of their friendship. On looking back it is possible to see some of the causes of this sad estrangement. Max was a democrat, and he believed that committees, whatever their limitations, were an essential element in arriving at democratic decisions. Leonard was an autocrat; he disliked committees, and was a bad chairman of them. Both of them enjoyed a battle, and did not mince their words when the argument was hot. But while it was possible to have a flaming row with Max without there being anything personal about it, Leonard was inclined to take it personally. Max was an able

160

administrator and played the game according to the rules. Leonard did his administration, but on the whole it bored him, and if he felt that the desired end could be reached by breaking the rules, he saw no reason against doing so. They were both liberal in their theological views, but while Max's liberalism was complex and cerebral, Leonard's was simple and pastoral. Both were warm-hearted and generous, but while Leonard was spontaneous in the expression of his emotions, Max was reserved about his own and inclined to be sceptical about other people's.

When Leonard and those he consulted had surveyed the needs of the diocese, it was decided to launch an appeal for £1,200,000. This was to meet the cost of new churches, combined churches and halls, sites, vicarages and halls, over the period of the next ten years. The appeal was launched in 1956. Three years later, a little over half this amount had been raised. In an interview published in *The Birmingham Post*, Leonard expressed his disappointment that the appeal, which he had originally hoped would reach its target in 1960, was hanging fire. Industrial and business sources had accounted for more than sixty per cent of the total subscribed. He acknowledged the generosity of many firms but said there were others who had done nothing after several approaches.

I am quite certain that there are firms who would respond if they could see the value of the churches they would help to build. I have always emphasised that the parish has the pastoral care of everyone in it, whatever their denomination. I still think it is within the compass of the diocese to help me get this amount cleared off, so that we can concentrate on the real work of the Church, of which bricks and mortar are only a part. I would like to go to the firms myself, but pressure of work is so great that I have to delegate the job and this does not seem to please some firms.

In the end, with the help of allocations from the Church Commissioners, Leonard got his total. It took some years to complete the appeal. Considering the general financial situation during most of those years, this was a great achievement. If Leonard had continued doing all the top personal contacts himself, as he had at the start of the appeal, he might have got his results more quickly. Managing directors expect to be called on by managing directors. Leonard knew how to get alongside them, and they liked seeing him. However, as he said, there were other claims on his time and Leonard, though he had been successfully involved in money-raising campaigns both for the Singapore diocese and for Manchester Cathedral, was not one of those who enjoyed them for their own sake. From the start Leonard was determined that the churches which were built should be large enough to seat four hundred, and Max Dunlop agreed with him on this. They were both keen on a church being able to accommodate the local schools for their annual services. Leonard said he was not going to be remembered as the bishop who built small churches. He was a whole-hearted supporter of the parochial system, which, he believed, could become again what it had been when he was one of the Town Moor parsons in Newcastle. 'We shall build for the future and for the congregations we are going to attract as time goes on.'

We are too near to the event to pass any final judgment on a strategy based on the parochial system. The cracks in it, which are obvious to many now, were not at all so apparent sixteen years ago. Leonard himself lost some of his enthusiasm as the appeal dragged out, but this did not change his belief that bricks and mortar had an essential part to play in that personal and pastoral work which was the real purpose of the Church's life.

V   GENERAL CONCERNS

The Hydrogen Bomb

When the Bill for the abolition of capital punishment was before the House of Lords, Leonard attended the debate and voted for the Bill. He did not speak in the debate. 'Afterwards,' he said to a friend, 'I wondered if I should have spoken. I think I am the only member who has been under sentence of death. It might have been helpful if I had told them what it felt like.'

Leonard played his part in the House of Lords, in Convocation and in the Church Assembly, and it is of interest to recall some of the subjects in the discussion of which he made an important contribution. The first of these was in a debate in Convocation in May 1954 on the hydrogen bomb. He began by pointing out that throughout the history of the Christian Church there had been two views about war. There was the absolute pacifist view which denied the right of any Christian to take up arms under any circumstances, and there was the view endorsed by a majority of the Churches that there was the right of a nation to defend itself if attacked, or to resort to force in the fulfilment of international obligations. He went on:

> The important thing to notice is that among Christians, Pacifists and non-Pacifists alike, all have agreed, and still do agree, that the claims of Christ are paramount, above and beyond all temporal loyalties, of state or country or party. Where we differ amongst ourselves is in the extent and the occasion of the use of physical force.

With this background he moved the first resolution, 'This Convocation regards the hydrogen bomb as a grievous enlargement of the evil inherent in all war, and as a threat to the basic obligations of humanity and civilisation.'

He went on to point out that there was an 'enlargement' when civilians became involved in what was total war; that modern inventions had made it possible to destroy all human life on the globe; that there was no escape from the dilemma of having to choose the lesser of two evils, for tyranny was also a threat to the basic obligations of humanity and civilisation. He continued:

> I know the ridicule that can be poured upon the nicely calculated less or more, but it seems to me to be unrealistic to

say that there is no difference between the hydrogen bomb and the bow and arrow. Both may be wrong, but the human misery and agony caused by the former is spread ten thousand times more than the hurts of the latter. All the atrocities and tortures of previous wars seem to pale beside the remembrance and the knowledge of those men, women, and children, obliterated in a few seconds, and the thousands crippled and maimed, existing sterile for a time, and then dying suddenly of the 'bomb sickness'. This we have already seen in Hiroshima, and the future agonies strain all sympathetic imagination.

Leonard went on to speak of the relationship between religion and politics, and the following passage represents his views then and generally throughout his life.

After experiment with and experience of the Church controlling the State, and the State controlling the Church, there developed the nineteenth-century theory of a free Church in a free State. The idea served its purpose for a time. The basic error, however, of this view has been demonstrated by the separation of spirit and matter. The Church was supposed to deal with spiritual things; the State with material things. The theory was supposed to be the political expression of 'Render to Caesar the things that are Caesar's, and to God the things that are God's'; but the conception of the relationship between the two has meant much less both to God and Caesar.

A truer conception could be expressed in the words, 'A freely influenced State sensitive to the presence of a morally commanding Church.' When it is spiritual the Church is the critic of every decision taken by the State, praising what is good, condemning what is evil. When the Church is alive with the moral, social and spiritual quality which it claims belongs to the life of God, it releases energies which are a divine gift to the State. The late Dr. Lindsay, Master of Balliol, if I understand him aright, made this point when he talked about the law of justice and the law of love. States are bound to govern and be governed by the law of justice, individuals are persuaded to be self-governed by the law of love; but individuals can so live their lives that they play the game better than the rules, and so enable the rules of justice to approximate nearer to the laws of love . . . Our Christian task is to be lifted, and to seek to lift mankind, away from the things that are seen and temporal to the things that are unseen and eternal; but this other-worldliness should not make us despair of the world, but rather encourage us to interpret these eternal values in the life of men and society. The fight before us today, and perhaps for generations to come, is to preserve that one seamless robe of Christ, the freedom of the natural soul. We seek a world where the natural soul can live. If, by the grace of God we can limit, control and redirect this new, God-given power, God will have given us a breathing space in which to carry out our major task, the evangelisation of the world.

Church members realise the danger of thinking that it is simple to apply Gospel insight and standards to the political order. We realise that there is a continual tension between Christian love and all political attempts to implement it. We stand, however, at the beginning, not the end, of the Church's adventure in this very complex world, at this critical moment in human history. So far, then, from suggesting that we have the answer as to how the intervention of God in the temporal order may take place, we emphasise again that our plea is precisely that the answer to that question will be given to the Church when it is more united and repentant, less preoccupied with merely saving the present situation, and much readier for a revolutionary adventure of faith.

Two years later, George Bell, Bishop of Chichester, wrote to Leonard asking him if he would support him in a motion on nuclear weapons he proposed to move in Convocation. This motion included the words, 'This House, noting the immense and indiscriminate destruction wrought by unlimited nuclear warfare, appeals to Her Majesty's Government to cease from all further tests of large-scale nuclear weapons, and to take the preliminary steps required for renouncing in advance the British Government's intention of ever being the first to use the hydrogen bomb.'

Leonard replied that he was sorry that he could not support the motion as it stood.

> I think the easing of the tension in the world situation is very largely due to the fact that we have nuclear weapons, and I cannot see that we can have them without testing them. But the only amendment that I would make would be to say, 'To seek all possible means to regulate tests', instead of 'To cease from all further tests'. This amendment is probably wholly unacceptable, but I would certainly support the rest of the resolution.
>
> Thank you for your confidence in inviting me to support you, and it grieves me that I cannot go all the way with you.

Two years later, at the Lambeth Conference in 1958, Greer, Bishop of Manchester, did his best to get the conference to outlaw the hydrogen bomb. Both Leonard and R. O. Hall supported Greer in this. Greer wanted the use of the bomb outlawed, not its retention. The resolution was intended as a religious act speaking for the conscience of Christian people. With ten more votes the resolution would have been carried. The fact that it was not was due to the votes of American bishops.

As time went on Leonard's views became stronger. In March 1967 there was a debate on disarmament in the House of Lords in which he spoke. He said that a Minister of the Crown was alleged to have said at the launching of the Polaris submarine that questions of decisions about deterrents were merely political and not moral questions, and that bishops did not come into it at all. Leonard said he could not accept that view. He believed there was a need for a State which was sensitive to and ready to understand some of the moral insights of a commanding and morally commanding Church. Whether or not the Church as they knew it could be rightly called a morally commanding Church was another question. But those who took their stand within that body had a duty and a right to speak on these matters. 'The fact that I happen to be a bishop does not mean that I can know nothing whatever about cricket or the World Cup.' It was the duty of those who cared to make themselves as knowledgeable as they could. The question whether these nuclear weapons were a deterrent was a moral as well as a political question. Leonard said that he shared the point of view of those who did not believe that these weapons were in fact a deterrent, and he thought the time had come to take a moral stand. They had been talking about the greatness of Britain. Surely a great part of that greatness lay in their willingness to take risks, in such a way as to say, 'We think it morally wrong to have these weapons. We want the other nations to give them up. We will begin.'

Divorce and Pastoral Care

In 1956 there came up for discussion in Convocation the report on the pastoral care of those who have remarried after divorce. Leonard and Canon Guy Warman submitted a minority report and Leonard spoke on this in the debate. He made it clear that he was in agreement with the majority of the committee on the main objectives; to uphold the principle of permanence in marriage, and to provide for the pastoral care of the individuals concerned where a remarriage had taken place after divorce. On the question of admission to Holy Communion, Leonard said:

> If our view is correct that reception is far more a means of grace than of pastoral discipline, then it is difficult to see the wisdom of a six months' 'quarantine'. Have we a right to say to anyone, 'You must not say your prayers for six months?' And are there not enough parallels between these two means of grace to make it dangerous and hurtful to say, 'You must

167

not receive the Sacrament?' If the offence of getting married again is open and notorious, at the end of six months it may be less notorious but it is equally, if not more, open.

Although Leonard's general motion was not carried, he was successful in getting taken out of the resolutions the proposed stipulation that a bishop should not give his consent to the readmission to communion of remarried couples unless they had lived in the diocese six months.

On the general question Leonard was committed to two points. He believed that the use of excommunication as a discipline of the Church was contrary to some of the sayings of Jesus. It was a very grave thing to deny 'the extraordinary drama of the forgiving love of God' to those in need of it. He said, 'We ought to rethink the whole question of using the Holy Communion as a disciplinary measure. It is a pastoral opportunity.' Leonard's other main point was that the matter was far better left in the hands of the parish priest, who should take counsel with his bishop if it was necessary. Leonard felt that the parish priest should be trusted. He would be nearest to the circumstances of each particular case and he was able to make continuing personal contact with the two people involved. He said, 'It is the parish priest who will have to give the pastoral care and express the law of love, with all its severity and all its tenderness. The parish clergy of England can still be entrusted with this ministry and most of them have no wish to escape it.'

However much he might disagree with the view of others in Bishops' Meetings, in Convocation, or in the Church Assembly, once a decision had been made, Leonard was always loyal to it. This did not prevent him from making his views known in an endeavour to help individuals, and to persuade people generally of the truth as he saw it. The problems raised by divorce were often in his mind, and following the debates in Convocation, he did a talk on the radio, and an article in *John Bull*. In this article Leonard referred to the resolutions of Convocation in 1938. The first affirmed that marriage, according to God's will, was essentially a union of one man with one woman exclusive of all others and indissoluble save by death. The second declared that divorce therefore always involved a departure from the true principle of marriage as declared by our Lord. The third resolution directed that to maintain the principle of lifelong obligation which is inherent in every legally contracted marriage and is expressed in the plainest terms in the marriage service, the Church should not allow the use of that service in the case of anyone who had a former partner still living. Leonard then went on:

> What can be done towards a Christian solution of this enormous problem of divorce and remarriage which faces the Church today?
> We have already seen the difficulty of deciding who is the innocent and who is the guilty party. Might it not be the right thing for the Church to allow remarriage to repentant parties, and only to them; that is to those who are truly sorry for their failure and turn to God for help? The parish clergyman to whom they go is far more likely to judge their sincerity rightly than is anyone else.

On the question of admission to communion, Leonard said he spoke for a minority group, which he hoped was growing.

> We regard the Convocation rule forbidding the marriage service in Church to anyone who has a former partner still living as a sad necessity, in an age when the standard of Christian marriage has been so widely disregarded; but we realise that this rule imposes a severe strain on the consciences of many clergymen. We would not wish, nor would we see any necessity, to add to this strain by rules of excommunication.
> We take the view that reception of Holy Communion is a means of grace, and therefore of enlightenment, and, holding as we do that a second marriage is not in itself adulterous, feel

that the responsibility of partaking unworthily rests on those who desire to come to communion, and that those who present themselves do so for commendable reasons . . . What needs to be kept in mind are the grave social and moral problems caused by divorce; and the Church should work with all possible agencies to prevent the breakdown of marriage. But when the tragedy has occurred, and the break, in human terms, is beyond repair, the Church should give every possible help by providing the assurance of God's grace to those who try to build a second married home.

Leonard showed the same kind of liberal attitude in a matter of pastoral care when Convocation was discussing infant baptism in 1965. At this date, there was a movement among some of the clergy to apply a much stricter discipline, and to refuse to baptise children unless they felt that parents and godparents were going to take their duties more seriously than was often the case. In some cases, individual clergy were making demands which went beyond the recommendations which had been carried by Convocation in 1957. In the Birmingham diocese the focus of this rigorist movement was in the rural deanery of Smethwick. Speaking in Convocation Leonard said that he found himself more and more holding the position of the Baptists. He thought it was more theologically honest. He would welcome a service of admission of infants, and he would like to see the appointment of a high-powered commission to re-examine the theological and pastoral problems of infant baptism. He felt that where every possible care was taken to see that parents recognised their obligations, that was enough, and incumbents ought not to refuse those who came in good faith. Parents and godparents might make mistakes. He thought they often did, but the clergy and congregations should help them to carry out their promises. In some cases baptism had been refused unless both parents were willing to attend a course of instruction in the Christian faith. Careful preparation was important but

170

there were limits. They were not detectives; they had to accept people's good faith. If they did not, they created an atmosphere of suspicion and despair about the Church, that it lacked compassion.

There was no doubt many in Convocation who agreed with Leonard, but he was always the champion of compassion against rigorism when these two were in conflict.

The Police and the Community

Leonard always felt involved in social questions of the day. It was seldom a day passed without a careful reading of the newspapers. In the opinion of one who worked very closely with him he really regarded this as a form of prayer. His years in Birmingham were marked by three problems in which he was very concerned and to which he gave much thought and effort. These were the relationship between the police and the community, the immigrant population, and the housing problem.

Early in 1964 an article on *The Church and the Police* was published in *Crucible*, the journal of the Board for Social Responsibility of the National Assembly of the Church of England. It was written by the Venerable L. G. Tyler who was then Archdeacon of Rochdale, and later became Principal of William Temple College. This article was very well informed and showed a sympathetic insight into the life and working conditions of the police. It was widely welcomed by the police, and as a result of discussions between the Board for Social Responsibility and high officers in the police service, the police invited the board to set up a group to consider some of the far-reaching questions raised in the archdeacon's article and nominated four of their own number to serve on this group. In October, Mr. Edwin Barker, the secretary to the board, wrote to Leonard asking him to become chairman of the group. The choice of the right chairman was vital to a successful carrying-out of the project. In the informal discussions which had taken place it was quite clear that Leonard's name met with the wholehearted support of the representatives of the police. He had excellent relations with their senior officials in Birmingham, who had complete confidence in his integrity and understanding. Leonard accepted the position and the first meeting took place in November.

The commission met eleven times, over a period of two and a half years and in April 1967 their report was published under the title *Police; A Social Study*. The report is a valuable document and it was widely read, the police themselves being the main purchasers when it first came out. At the beginning of the commission's work the police were very much on the defensive. It was eighteen months before this was broken down, and the fact that good and easy relations were established was largely due to Leonard's chairmanship. His humanity and his humour won the respect and confidence of the members of the commission. This was his main contribution to the work, and it was a vital one; there were others who could supply the necessary expert knowledge. He did, however, contribute a paper for the second meeting which considered the nature of the authority of the State. This was based on a lecture of Hastings Rashdall under the title *Ideas and Ideals* which Leonard reduced and reordered to provide a basis for discussion. The great value of the commission's work was that it established an active liaison between the police, clergy, social workers, head teachers and others with a concern for the relations between the police and the community. Regular courses in which police, clergy and others took part were established under Leonard Tyler when he was appointed principal of William Temple College. These still go on, and have now been attended by representatives from every police force in the country.

Leonard enjoyed this work. He felt that here was something which could become a substantial help in a changing society. He very much liked the personal contacts which arose out of the commission. When the report had been issued, and the continuing work was entrusted to a committee of the British Council of Churches, Leonard insisted that the group who had made up the commission should go on meeting informally after its last official meeting, and it did in fact do so until Leonard's death.

Immigrants and Housing

In 1959 Leonard appointed Paul Burrough, now Bishop of Mashonaland, to be his Chaplain for Overseas Peoples. Burrough first met Leonard in Malaya. After ten weeks of the war, he was back in Singapore and on several occasions had breakfast with Leonard and John Hayter after service at the cathedral. They were all three together in Leonard's house when the first air-raid on Singapore took place. In 1959, Burrough was sent back to England from Korea on doctor's orders and Leonard got in touch with him at once. What followed is best told in Burrough's own words.

Leonard asked me if I would go and work with him in Birmingham. He was prepared to offer me a parish, or the opportunity of working among immigrants because he had set up a chaplaincy but never filled it. He took meticulous care to try not to take me away from other work. I thought it right to work with him, and after a number of meetings and telephone messages in his usual humble and courteous way, I agreed that I would go and be his Chaplain to Overseas Peoples. I remember when I first discussed this with him, and told him that I intended to live in a caravan and move about among the twenty or so parishes where coloured people were living, he said, 'The Christian ministry has to be done in many different ways; if that's the way you want to do it, then of course I give it my blessing.' He went on to say, 'I shall never ask reports or results from you. I merely want you to show something of the love of God to these people in the streets of Birmingham who move my heart with their great need.'

Leonard took great interest in my work, and would sometimes come to my caravan, or go out visiting with me for a couple of hours round the homes of immigrants. At other times he was prepared to speak at meetings, and in every way

173

followed his great sense of compassion for the immigrants of Birmingham. He did this with a practical and real approach which did not minimise the problems of colour or race, but showed that, above all, his concern was for the Christian ministry of reconciliation. It was Leonard who enabled me to make a visit to the West Indies so that I could learn more about the homes of the people among whom I worked, and finally, he asked me to be a residentiary canon at the cathedral because he wanted to mark in the diocese the importance of the work among the immigrant population which had then reached about ninety thousand. When he got back from a rather terrifying visit to Biafra during the war there, he came and spoke wonderfully to a gathering of Biafran people, fifty or sixty of them, in a hall at Christchurch, Summerfield.

In March 1965, Leonard took part in a debate in the House of Lords on the problems of immigration. He pointed out that Birmingham was one of the places where these arose in their acutest form. Taking the area covered by the diocese the coloured population amounted to ten per cent of the whole. He said that he himself could see no alternative to some form of control, but it was important to see that the control was exercised in the best possible way. There were three factors that ought to be taken into account. Immigrants must have a clean bill of health; they must have a job to come to; and there ought to be some kind of preparation in their own country before they came as to what they were likely to come to. He went on to plead that when consideration was given to the limits set upon a particular family, it would be a great mistake to cut off all the older generation. If they did so, they would be removing one of the stabilising forces in the immigrant community.

On the positive side Leonard said there ought to be a more general recognition of the amount of good the immigrants had done, and of the fact that their gifts were an enrichment to British society. The Health Service, the Transport Services and others could not get on without them. There ought also to be a re-examination of the housing problem from the point of view of the immigrants. There was no special provision for them. They had to take their place in the queue, and in Birmingham there were in fact no houses available for an extra population. He said he knew of cases where Indians and Pakistanis had bought up houses and were letting them out at rents of £2 5s 0d to £3 15s 0d a room to whole families of West Indians and Irish. In many cases such families were sharing a kitchen and toilet with six other families. He had seen for himself the conditions and had had meals with these people in going from one room to another. It was equally necessary to face the educational problem. The Commonwealth Advisory Council had suggested that not more than one third of the numbers in any school should be coloured. In many schools in the Midlands the number was half, and in some practically the whole school was coloured.

The problem of immigration and the problem of housing were closely related in Birmingham, and Leonard made it his business to be well informed about both. One of the most telling speeches he made was in a debate in the House of Lords in 1962 on housing and land prices. The speech was very well received in the Lords and gave enormous satisfaction to Birmingham Corporation. He had been well briefed by Canon Ralph Stevens, his industrial chaplain, and he had made himself master of the essential facts and figures. He said there were thirty thousand families in Birmingham living in lodgings, and hundreds of cases where a husband and wife with three or four children were living in one room without kitchen or living-room and having to share kitchen and toilet with other families. There were forty-seven thousand other families living in homes of their own, which had been condemned as unfit for human habitation. Birmingham had built forty thousand new houses since the war, and could not build faster than at the then rate of two thousand two hundred houses a year. The work was impeded by the high cost of building workers' wages and the slowness of the Government in allocating land for building purposes. The public conscience needed to be aroused on these matters, and perhaps one way of doing so was to make the public pay more towards the cost of the work. One of the evils of the situation arose from the fact that as families grew, the tension in the home often became unbearable under these overcrowded conditions. Families were broken up when the younger members were forced out and had to live in hostels. This was a grave moral problem which had a dangerously destructive effect on the life of the community.

Remembrance Day

In November 1967, a year before the fiftieth anniversary of the first Armistice Day, Leonard moved a resolution in the Church Assembly about Remembrance Day. The gist of the motion was that the time had come for a reassessment of its purpose and that it was important to ask both what to remember and how to remember. Leonard said:

> The French have always said that the faculty of forgetfulness is a national failing in England. He might perhaps reply that such forgetfulness is better than bitter memories, but best of all are the memories which are not bitter but ennobling. We are bidden in the New Testament to forget the things that are behind, yet we are also bidden to call to remembrance the former times. In spite of their contradictory appearance, both these biddings are true and both are important. Most of the western world tried to keep alive the memory of great men and great events by public monuments and commemorations. Monuments as well as cathedrals have kindled the imagination of both young and old, and the influence of war memorials has been neither slight nor degrading.
>
> Although commonly called war memorials, they do not commemorate the glories and triumphs of war, but are records of human valour and suffering, and they silently attest the truth that lies in our Lord's words, 'Greater love hath no

man than this, that a man lay down his life for his friends.'
The fact that some of them knew at the time, and many more
of us have come to see later, the stupidity and futility of war,
does not diminish but rather enhances their nobility and
greatness.

In the first thirty years the commemoration of Armistice
Day round these memorials was poignant with sacred
memories of deeply loved relatives and friends, and there was
a sadness mingled with our proud thanksgiving and also with
our Christian hope and confidence in our reunion with them.
There was something more: a dedication to live more bravely
for the sake of those no longer with us. The struggle is now
to secure justice, fellowship, faith and peace among mankind . . . In taking up this struggle . . . we are keeping faith
with those we commemorate on Remembrance Day.

Next year will be the fiftieth anniversary of the first
Armistice Day, and suggestions are being voiced that the
time has come to abolish the official observance of Remembrance Day. We are told that to the young people, for whom
the two world wars are not even a memory, the ceremonies
are meaningless. I would say there was certainly not enough
evidence to justify a change. Such evidence as we have from
interrogation on television of people of all ages was strongly
in favour of the retention in some form of a Day of
Remembrance.

He went on to say that he would welcome a change of
emphasis so that the note of thanksgiving in the services held
should include acts of self-sacrifice in every field of life, and
there should be a more contemporarily relevant expression of
penitence and dedication.

May I end by saying something about the British Legion
Service which is held annually at the Albert Hall. Although
it has been televised for many years, it still remains quite
rightly the service of the British Legion, and therefore can

have its own particular emphasis; but it is worth reminding the public that the service is ecumenical and is conducted by the Free Churches, the Roman Catholic Church, and the Church of England. At that service we thank God for men and women of all nations and of every age who have suffered or given their lives for truth and freedom.

For many years Leonard took the annual Service of Remembrance and Reunion for the Far Eastern Prisoners of War Association held in the Royal Festival Hall. He had been connected with the association since his time in Manchester. Mr. E. J. Coffey, Deputy Chairman of the National Federation of Far Eastern Prisoners of War Clubs, writes:

He was always known as 'Our Bishop', and was greatly loved by all Far Eastern prisoners-of-war irrespective of race or creed.

Probably one of the most significant things happened after his death, when the Emperor of Japan paid an official visit to this country. Many of our members took great exception to this, but at our annual conference held in Buxton last May it was agreed that we would take no action. This was mainly due to the conference being reminded of the teachings we had so often heard the bishop tell us.

CHAPTER 10

The Last Years

By the end of his years in Birmingham Leonard was beginning to feel the strain. This is hardly surprising. He was seventy in November 1967, and he had had a very active life. However, there was still plenty of drive and spirit in him. In an interview for the *Sunday Times Magazine* in December 1967 he said:

> There was more independence among vicars when I was ordained. These days your clergy will ask you questions that one decided for oneself as a curate. Understandable, I suppose. People's liberty is disappearing all the time with all these rules and regulations about. In the old days there was no hullabaloo about giving communion to people who had been divorced. If you felt there was a good case you'd just do it.

This was the same man as had always been there. And when, in the interview, he was gently quizzed about his reputation as a jolly bishop who liked going to pubs and was for ever making jokes, his comment was equally characteristic:

> One has a certain amount of tolerance. Pubs are good places to get people to think about God. There's always a great deal of fellowship about. I don't like pub-crawling much myself. I do like bridge and travelling on Swiss trains. Well, they're very clean and you just sit there and look at the tremendous views, and at the stations you can get out and walk about.

Leonard was made a K.C.M.G. in the 1968 New Year's Honours, and the year that followed was as busy as most. In March he went to Biafra. He left at a week's notice, at the invitation of the Archbishop of Canterbury, in company with the Archbishop of West Africa, a representative of the Methodist Church and one of the Church of Scotland. He was well aware of the dangers, but he went off in great spirits like an undergraduate on his first adventure abroad. Shortly after he got home, Leonard wrote to his son, Timothy, in South America, describing some of his experiences:

The object of the exercise was to take a message of goodwill to the Churches there. It was partly to keep up with the Joneses because the Vatican had sent out a delegation from Rome. It was an exciting journey to get there. We had to go to Lisbon first. Then after waiting more than twenty-four hours we transferred at 2 a.m. to a German gun-running plane with American pilots run by some charter company. The twelve seats in the rear of the plane were comfortable enough but there were very few amenities. After ten hours in the plane we came down in what I understand is the Rio Pongas Bissau (or some name like that). Here we had a meal; delicious rolls, but butter like crude oil. After two hours, we embarked again, and, after six or seven hours, we tried to land at Port Harcourt. All our lights, including navigation lights, had been extinguished, and after sitting silently in the dark for two hours we were told we couldn't get the proper radio signals, and therefore had to go on to San Toma, a Portuguese island on the equator.

It was midnight before we got there, and 1 a.m. before we got a cheese sandwich and a beer at a hotel with no air-conditioning. Still, I was so tired I slept well, and as we could only get to Port Harcourt in the dark, we had to wait twenty-four hours before making the next attempt. This time we were successful, but customs and immigration formalities took so long that it was nearly midnight when we sat down to a Government dinner of about a hundred people. Here we were guests of the Biafran Government. A first-class hotel with V.I.P. treatment, and it was clear the Government was going to dictate where and how we went. Everywhere we went we were met by huge crowds and an address of welcome (so called). All the placards were anti-British. The Prime Minister was once called 'Mr. Leonard Wilson', and I had to listen to a long tirade about the iniquities of a double-faced State, which supplied arms to their enemies, and a Church equally responsible for the bombs and showing callous indifference to the sufferings of their fellow Christians in Biafra. I told them that very few people in England had heard of Biafra and those who had thought it was an Italian football team. The Press and the B.B.C. were attacked for their complete silence about Biafra and their lying accounts from Lagos about the successes of the Federal troops. I learnt to control my temper all the time, and my tongue part of the time. We were usually going from 7.30 a.m. to midnight, travelling in good cars with jeeps as escorts and fully armed guards. We had to see many craters at every stop. We were able to go to the churches on Sunday but there was often a service at the big meetings. They were ingenious in choosing psalms like, 'Fret not thyself thou tyrant that thou canst do mischief,' with lessons about Judas betraying the innocent blood and losing his thirty pieces of silver.

In spite of all this day after day, my sympathies are entirely with the Biafrans, who have suffered before the war over thirty thousand massacred, and more than one million losing their homes and possessions on being driven from the North. If this is all the security that the Federation can give them no wonder they wanted to secede (the spelling doesn't look right but I haven't time to look it up). At one time I wondered if I would ever get out of the country. We had to get under the table at one meeting when a plane came over,

181

but no bomb was dropped. After five days of travelling hundreds of miles, and having scores of argy-bargys, and listening to countless addresses of welcome, I felt years younger. There was no personal animosity to us; a very great deal of kind hospitality and genuine gratitude for our visit, but I was glad to be safely back having been ten days away, five days being taken up with the journey.

At the end of April Leonard spoke in the House of Lords in a debate on the cease-fire proposals for Nigeria. He said that in his recent visit to Biafra he had been at pains to try to find out whether in fact the bombs being dropped by the Federal forces were of British manufacture. He had told those in authority whom he had seen that if he was to act as their advocate on his return he must have the truth; he must have evidence which would stand up in a court of law. They had not given him such evidence. He had seen the bomb casings inscribed with the words 'made in Britain' and saw the letters 'GE—' cut off, these being the first two letters of the word 'Gelignite'. He also saw that these letters could not have been stuck on, as the surface of the casings was clearly and precisely indented to correspond with the letters. Leonard had suggested that the bombs had perhaps come from another nation which had bought them from Britain. The Biafrans had claimed that this could not be so. Turning to the question of the minorities, Leonard said he thought the crucial test had been put to him by Colonel Ojukwu. What had happened when minority areas were invaded? Instead of falling into the arms of the Federal soldiers and greeting them as liberators, the inhabitants had retreated towards Biafra. How could they federate when there had been such terrible massacre of the civilian population through the bombing raids. Leonard ended by suggesting that it would have a deep psychological effect on the situation if Britain was to say, 'It is time you got together, and until you do we are are not going to send any more arms.' The opposing forces must come together without conditions and he believed Colonel Ojukwu was ready to accept that.

In such spare time as they could find, Leonard and Mary were looking round for a place where they might make their home when he retired. They eventually found a house in Wensleydale, near the village of Askrigg, which they decided to buy and alter to their needs. In the autumn he saw a specialist as he was finding any hard walking difficult. He had a form of cramp caused by damage to the arteries of his legs. The specialist advised against an operation. He did not think it would get any worse, and otherwise Leonard was in very sound health for a man of his age.

The year followed its usual pattern of work inside and outside the diocese. In June, Paul Burrough was consecrated Bishop of Mashonaland in Birmingham Cathedral. A number of African bishops were present who were in England for the Lambeth Conference. Local history was made when Leonard and the Roman Catholic Archbishop of Birmingham, Dr. Dwyer, walked together in the robed procession. With the departure of Burrough there came to an end a close association which had meant much to them both. The choice of Burrough to be his Chaplain for Overseas People was one of the best and happiest appointments Leonard made. They had taken to one another at sight, when they had first met in Malaya, and in the years while Burrough was working in Birmingham, the friendship deepened. Leonard recognised how well this special work had been done, but, more than that, he greatly appreciated the wise counsel and spiritual comfort Burrough gave to him. He missed him all the more because during recent years a number of his personal friends of long standing had died, including Kenneth Parsons, Max Dunlop, Frank Atkinson, Jock Malcolm and Eric Featherstone.

The Lambeth Conference involved the usual heavy programme. When the bishops went to different dioceses for the missionary weekend, which was held in the middle of the conference, Bishop Baker was among the party which went to Birmingham. He recalls that they had a busy but not too hectic programme, and on one of the evenings Leonard arranged for his guests to be invited to dinner and the theatre at Stratford-on-Avon. The play was *Troilus and Cressida*, and when Baker remarked to Leonard that although it was not Shakespeare at his best, it perhaps had its message as an indictment of contemporary society, Leonard said, 'Yes, lechery and war, lechery and war, that was all.' Bishop Baker also remembers another Shakespearean reference. At one of the meetings at the conference an American bishop had criticised something he, Baker, had said, as being out of order, or not on the subject. The Archbishop of Canterbury had come to his defence in an unexpectedly spirited fashion. Shortly afterwards in the coffee break, Leonard commented on this, saying, 'Who would have thought the old man to have had so much blood in him?'

Leonard did not play a very active part in the conference debates, though there is a characteristic utterance recorded in *The Long Shadow of Lambeth*,* when the question of the ordination of women was under discussion.

> The Bishop of Birmingham said wearily, 'I cannot see why women should not have their place in the ministry of Christ as deacons, priests or bishops . . . I can't help but think of the time when the early Church had to decide whether to let in the Gentiles.'

Leonard was President of the Anglican Group for the Ordination of Women. He was much appreciated by that body for his wise counsel and for the fact that he was courageous in commending its cause when few diocesan bishops were prepared to do so.

In January 1969, Leonard wrote to the Prime Minister saying that he would like to resign as from September 30th. This was

* *The Long Shadow of Lambeth* by J. B. Simpson and E. M. Story. McGraw-Hill Book Company.

not formally announced until March 1st. In the meantime, Leonard accepted an invitation from the B.B.C. to go out to Singapore to make a television programme on his experiences at the time of his internment. In 1959 the Rank Organisation had made a film about this entitled *Singapore Story*. Leonard took Ralph Stevens to see this, and afterwards asked him what he thought of it. Stevens said, 'I did not dislike it as much as I thought I would. But it wasn't you. It was humourless.' Leonard replied, 'That's what I thought.' The film was in fact very much in demand for a considerable time, but for those who knew Leonard it was not right. The attempt to combine television documentary material and acted material is seldom satisfactory.

Leonard and Mary flew to Singapore, where they were to be met at the airport by the producer, Derek Smith, and Canon William Purcell, who was to do the commentary and the interviewing for the programme. Purcell and Leonard had often worked together before, when the former had been the B.B.C. Religious Organiser for the Midland Region. Purcell recalls the moving reception given to the Wilsons when they landed,

When we got to the airport, we found quite a number of elderly, or any at rate late-middle-aged Asiatics, Chinese and Malay, including some clergy, waiting around. When the plane landed and Wilson came down the steps, there ensued an astonishing and quite unrehearsed scene. They waved to him from the barriers, and as he came out of the customs, they were very moved. Elizabeth Choy, in particular, who had been in a cell with him for many months during the war, knelt down and kissed his hand, the tears streaming down her face. Many of the others were also strongly moved. Indeed, the commotion was such that a very young Singapore policeman came up to me and the following conversation ensued. The policeman asked, 'Who is this man?' I replied, 'His name is Wilson and he was Bishop of Singapore during the war.' The policeman answered, 'What war? I don't know about any war. He is holding up the traffic.' A pretty ironical comment, I should have thought.

At the conclusion of the film called *Mission to Hell*, Purcell said, 'You describe these times we've been retracing as the golden years of your life!' Leonard answered:

Did I ever use such exaggerated language! I must learn to control it. I would have said that these times in Singapore were some of the richest spiritually that I have ever known. Opinions, however right, are mere prejudices unless they spring from a living root in your own experience. Now I had been taught things, the Church had taught me things, my parents had taught me things, the Bible had taught me things. I had tested some of them but never had I really known. But since those experiences here when I say I believe in, I hold Him dear, I can now say like St. Paul says, 'We know in whom we have believed.' The point was not the fact that I had to have this experience in order to know. The point was that that experience made me trust God and the trust in God was the thing that really mattered.

In April, the Knutsford Fellowship held its Jubilee Reunion at Saltley College. Leonard never forgot his debt to Knutsford. It was largely due to him that the meeting was residential. Nine years earlier there had been a reunion in London, but this had been only a day meeting, and at the time Leonard wrote a note putting down his disappointment at this limitation. This reveals some of Leonard's feelings about the Fellowship:

On reflection I found the Knutsford gathering both stimulating and frustrating, if you can bear that much over-used word.

To begin with I had met earlier in the day my old friend Jock Malcolm, who has been out of England for so long a time. I told him of the reunion and succeeded in persuading him to come, if only for a short time. He told me he didn't like 'ghosts'. (Most of them had fairly substantial bodies!) But the word haunted me a little, and the nostalgia created by the resurgence of a long-lost love was combined with other emotions. Why so few of my own year? What could the later ones know of the exhilaration of that first miraculous year? What could I know of the joys and inspiration of Hawarden where I had never resided? What was it that kept us together? Only when we heard again the prophetic voices of our pastors and masters of those far-off days, did we feel again the eternal element of our temporary abode of forty years ago. But there was not enough time to savour the feeling. If there is to be another such gathering, cannot we stay in one place and not scatter all over London?

Some may think there is a danger of sentimentality in such reunions, but the joy of true fellowship of sight and hand is a sentiment of which we need not be ashamed. I personally was refreshed in spirit by meeting the 'ghosts', and genuinely thankful to those who worked to make it possible, and to those who by their words rekindled the divine flames on the mean altars of our hearts.

For what we have received may the Lord make us truly thankful.

In July the clergy of the diocese assembled at Swanwick for a three-day conference. This was the third of these residential conferences for his clergy that Leonard called together during his time in Birmingham. It was his farewell to his clergy. It was at the final service that Leonard for the first time told them as a body of his wartime experiences in Singapore. As one who was present said afterwards, it was an unforgettable experience to see them troop back into the main building in complete silence, many of them having been in tears.

The official farewell from the city and the diocese took place in the Town Hall on September 24th. The Bishop of Aston spoke for the diocese and made the presentation.

Thus the Wilsons came to leave the house in Harborne which had been their home for sixteen years, where they had had so many gatherings of family and friends. Leonard was going back to the North, not indeed to his beloved County Durham, but near enough to have the feeling of home, and to a place whose natural beauty and friendly inhabitants were equally welcome to him. He shared in the village life and in the worship of the village church, and because he felt at ease with his new neighbours, they soon felt at ease with him.

In May, the Wilsons went to Guernsey for Leonard to preach at the twenty-fifth anniversary of the liberation of the Channel Islands from the Germans, and in June he took the chair at the Jubilee meeting of the Hong Kong Diocesan Association. This was the last public meeting that Leonard went to, and the words with which he ended his speech are a fitting last quotation.

> There is just one thing that I want to say: I love the Collect for St. John the Baptist's day; I like the advice 'constantly speak the truth, patiently suffer for the truth's sake'; glorious things, but we must remember that we live in a new covenant where we are no longer in the desert, and we have received from God some gracious promises. John the Baptist played at funerals; Jesus played at weddings, and there was a very great joy in all that He did. He delighted in the friendships, and although there must always be a puritan streak about our religion it is not that that has the final word. The final word is 'where the spirit of the Lord is, there is liberty', and to know how to abound as well as to be in want, and to give thanks for all the lovely things of life as well as thanking God for the pains and sorrows that we have. He is a God who wants us to enjoy Him for ever, as the Scottish catechism has it, and as well as our discipline there should be a great joy, and this Association is a very great joy.

On July 23rd he took his last service for the Order of St. Michael and St. George in St. Paul's Cathedral. His conduct of the service was always greatly appreciated and this was regarded by some of those present as the best he had ever taken.

In the train, on the way back to Yorkshire, he was taken ill. Happily his daughter, who is a doctor, was with him, and was able to take charge of the situation until he reached home. He had had a mild stroke, but this was followed almost at once by a second more serious one, causing partial paralysis. He was taken to Northallerton Hospital where he lay for several weeks, but when the possibility of recovery seemed to be past, he was taken to his home in Wensleydale, and he died there on August 18th.

Epilogue

THE MEMORIAL STONE to Leonard in Birmingham Cathedral is set into the floor at the foot of the chancel steps, where marriage couples stand. It bears this inscription:

JOHN LEONARD WILSON

1897 – 1970

FOURTH BISHOP OF BIRMINGHAM

SOMETIME BISHOP OF SINGAPORE

CONFESSOR FOR THE FAITH

Both the place and the words are fitting. A love of home and family and friends was deep-rooted in his heart, and he was, in truth, a confessor for the faith. His religion and his humanity went hand in hand, each deriving strength and depth from the other. Both were simple in character and quality, rich and spontaneous in feeling, vivid and warm in expression. He knew in his own experience the strengths and the weaknesses of human nature, and he saw both as falling within the circle of the divine grace. He had a wholeness of vision, and if at times he felt sad and frustrated when it was blurred and broken by events, he never lost hope in the triumph of the Christian faith and of the truth which would make men free.

Index